TYPOGRAPHY NOW TWO

imagine

TYPOGRAPHY NOW TWO

EDITED BY RICK POYNOR

implosion

First published in 1996
by Booth-Clibborn Editions
12 Percy Street
London W1P 9FB

Copyright © 1996 Rick Poynor

ISBN 1873968 612

Published and distributed in the United Kingdom

Worldwide direct mail rights:
Internos Books
12 Percy Street
London W1P 9FB
England

Trade distributors for the rest of the world:
Hearst Books International

Trade distributors in the USA:
F & W Publications Inc.

Printed and bound in Hong Kong by Dai Nippon Printing Co.

EDITOR, COMPILER AND WRITER	RICK POYNOR
ASSISTANT EDITOR	EMILY KING
ART DIRECTORS	JONATHAN BARNBROOK
	STEPHEN COATES
COVER, INTRODUCTION AND DIVIDER PAGE DESIGN	JONATHAN BARNBROOK
PAGE DESIGN	JASON BEARD

Sources for divider page quotations

PAGES 16/17

John Plunkett
"Plugged in"
Metropolis, October 1994

Joshua Berger
"Regarding the design, typography and legibility of this publication"
Plazm no. 6, 1994

Tobias Frere-Jones
"Towards the cause of grunge"
Zed no. 1, 1994

Rudy VanderLans
"Radical commodities"
Emigre no. 34, Spring 1995

Jan van Toorn
Thinking design: issues in culture and values
Western Carolina University, 1993

PAGES 78/79

P. Scott Makela
quoted in Michael Rock
"P. Scott Makela is wired"
Eye no. 12 vol. 3, 1994

Katherine McCoy
interviewed by Rick Poynor
Eye no. 16 vol. 4, 1995

Jonathan Barnbrook
interviewed by Rick Poynor
Eye no. 15 vol. 4, 1994

PAGES 106/107

Edward Fella
letter to Rick Poynor, 1995

Lorraine Wild
quoted in Anne Burdick
"A sense of rupture"
Eye no. 14 vol. 4, 1994

Louise Sandhaus
"An introduction from the designer of this journal"
Errant Bodies, Winter 1994

J. Abbott Miller,
"Must books be ugly, too?"
AIGA Journal of Graphic Design
vol. 11 no. 2, 1993

PAGES 182/183

Brian Schorn
letter to Rick Poynor, 1995

Michael Worthington
Hypertype, featured on California Institute of the Arts' 25th Anniversary CD-ROM, 1995

Jeffery Keedy
Fast Forward
California Institute of the Arts, 1993

FR

The five years that have passed since first publication of this book's predecessor, Typography Now: The Next Wave,

have seen the mainstreaming of experimental approaches to typography

that were until quite recently much more likely to be identified with "hothouse" design schools, or obscure arts journals with tiny circulations, than with the contents of the commercial break or the newsstand magazine. In 1991, when *Typography Now* was in preparation, such work, even within the design community, seemed to be a minority taste. Interesting as it was to observers like myself, it still came as a genuine surprise that a publisher was prepared to put out a book that concentrated – to the exclusion of all other forms of typography – on what many regarded as a wholly ignorable lunatic fringe.

BY RICK POYNOR

EEZING

¶*Typography Now Two*'s purpose is therefore both different from the first book's, and the same. It is different in the sense that, while I hope the book contains many unfamiliar examples, work of this kind is by now sufficiently familiar as a genre, even to those who still don't like it, not to require any special introduction (explanation is another matter). Whether it is seen as a regrettable fad that will eventually pass when the deluded finally see sense, or as an established and legitimate design method with plenty of remaining potential, **the "new typography" can no longer be said to be especially shocking – within the design profession, at least – or even particularly new. And, like any cultural form that sets out to kick over the traces, only to find itself applauded for the effort, its less thoughtful manifestations are subject to the law of diminishing returns.**

¶What *Typography Now Two* does share with its predecessor is a documentary intention. Enough time has elapsed for significant developments to have occurred and this book attempts to chart them. One of the most immediate differences in putting it together was the sheer volume of material to choose from five years on. The first wave of experimentally inclined typographers, whose careers began in the 1980s or earlier, have been joined in the 1990s by countless others inspired by their example. Designers who were undergraduates in 1991 now have work experience or second degrees behind them. The effect of earlier influences is noticeable at an institution such as London's Royal College of Art. It wasn't until the college's 1995 degree show that a marked sense of engagement with typographic concerns dating back anything from five to ten years in the United States surfaced across the body of student work. To give a sense of where typography may be heading in the next few years, this book looks at postgraduate work from the Royal College of Art, Cranbrook Academy of Art and, perhaps the most significant centre of new typography in the 1990s, California Institute of the Arts.

Press advertisement
Designer: Geof McFetridge
Client: California Institute
of the Arts
USA, 1994-95

Student project on the
Kennedy assassination
Designer: Carlo Tartaglia
Royal College of Art
Great Britain, 1995

Cover of *Climax* no. 1
Designers: Alessandro Manfredi,
Fabrizio Schiavi
Client: Happy Books
Italy, 1995

¶Given the international dimension and scale of these developments (which are still under way) no claims to definitiveness can be made for a collection of this size. *Typography Now Two* aims instead to give a selective but representative account of the experimental typography that characterised the period and a picture of some of the key ideas that accompanied it. The book shows significant minor projects that have a particular story to tell, or simply deserve to be better known, alongside more familiar examples, such as *Emigre* or *Raygun*, which must, by any reckoning, be regarded as central to typographic change in the 1990s.

¶These changes have not been accomplished without loud cries of pain from some sections of the design community.

Even as the first *Typography Now* was going to press, Massimo Vignelli was publicly blasting *Emigre* as a "factory of garbage". "That is a national calamity. It's not a freedom of culture, it's an aberration of culture . . . They show no responsibility. It's just like freaking out, in a sense. The kind of expansion of the mind that they're doing is totally uncultural."[1] Two years later, Paul Rand pitched in against "indecipherable, zany typography; tiny type with miles of leading; text in all caps (despite indisputable proof that lowercase letters are more readable, less formal, and friendlier); ubiquitous letterspacing; visually annotated typography; revivalist caps and small caps; pseudo Dada and Futurist collages; and whatever 'special effects' a computer makes possible."[2]

Poster for "New Typography" exhibition
Designer: Zsolt Czakó
Hungary, 1994

THE

¶If that didn't seem to leave many options open to the would-be typographic rebel, New York art director Henry Wolf was even more specific. He singled out a particular offender for detailed stylistic rebuttal, P. Scott Makela's *Living Surfaces* poster (reproduced on page 97), doubting "that history will repeat itself here".[3] But the most sustained and incisive attack on the perceived excesses of the new typography came from Steven Heller in his now notorious essay "Cult of the ugly". Heller's polemic triggered a fusillade of angry letters from supporters of typographic experimentation on both sides of the Atlantic and inspired an issue of *Emigre* (taken to task in the essay) devoted to probing Heller, eliciting the responses of some of those he had criticised, and clearing up what the magazine believed to be a misunderstanding of the purpose and context of the new design.[4]

Advertisement in *Blur* magazine
Designer: Scott Clum
Client: FontShop Canada
USA, 1993

¶The irony of these attacks was that it was already too late. While conservative critics focused on work produced within the insulated sanctum of the academy, or aimed at other designers, hotly contesting its relevance to the "real world", the genie of typographic inspiration (or vandalism, depending on your point of view) was already at large in the culture. The first issue of *Raygun*, art directed by David Carson, appeared in November 1992 and the magazine's immediate North American impact and rapport with its young readership helped to confirm and consolidate advertising and communication trends that had been gathering momentum since the 1980s. *Raygun*'s pyrotechnic type treatments, much like those of *The Face* ten years earlier, appeared to offer a fail-safe set of graphic codes for reaching a generation – "Generation X", as the novelist Douglas Coupland dubbed it – increasingly unmotivated by conventional means of address.

¶The difference, this time round, was that the advertising agencies did not dilute the message by making their own pale copies, as they had with Neville Brody's work in the mid-1980s. They bought the product straight from source. Nike's US agency, Wieden & Kennedy, was one of the first to set a premium on fashionable type by calling in Brody himself to help sell training shoes in 1988. In Europe, in the 1990s, Nike has commissioned type-led campaigns by Why Not Associates, David Carson and the London-based multidisciplinary team Tomato. Robert Nakata, a Cranbrook Academy of Art-educated typographer known

for boldly experimental projects at Studio Dumbar, left the Hague-based company to join Wieden & Kennedy's Amsterdam office, where he has created print campaigns for Nike and Microsoft. **At the same time, designers of high-impact type effects have forged an emotive new genre of ambient typography in their contributions to television commercials, pop promos and other moving-image projects, initially as typographers, but increasingly as directors, too.**

Outdoor brand campaign
Designer: Robert Nakata
Agency: Wieden & Kennedy
Client: Nike Europe
The Netherlands, 1992

Video for the song "Cowgirl"
Directors: Graham Wood, Robert Shackleton
Design company: Tomato
Client: Underworld
Great Britain, 1993

In Britain, Tomato, Why Not Associates and Jonathan Barnbrook probably have the highest profile; David Carson, Barry Deck and P. Scott Makela are perhaps the most strongly identified with the movement in the United States.

¶Type and typography are receiving more public attention in 1996 than at any previous time. The worldwide explosion, in the wake of Emigre Fonts, of small independent type foundries firing off little catalogues offering faces made with Fontographer that run the gamut from sublime to ridiculous has helped to put typographic design on the media map. David Carson is probably the only graphic designer at this point whose celebrity can command television coverage or a profile in *Newsweek*, but it is still not uncommon in the 1990s for *Esquire* to run an article on the grunge font phenomenon, for *Wired* to profile type designers Barry Deck and Jonathan Hoefler, or for a newspaper such as the *Chicago Tribune* to take a long, hard look at local goings-on in the typographic undergrowth – which led it to conclude, with laudable balance, that "New fonts have something to say, even if you can't always read them."[5]

Press advertisement for Foster's Ice beer
Designer: Cornel Windlin
Creative director: Ian Swift
Client: Scottish Courage
Great Britain, 1996

¶A telling instance of the emerging media belief that typography and the people who produce it are interesting to non-designers (or ought to be) came in a recent advertisement designed by Cornel Windlin for Foster's Ice beer. The double-page ad, a fractured collage of broken type and Macintosh screen commands, appears to mock its own claim to offer – in its own words – a "subversive appeal to 18-24 year olds". The ironic foregrounding of the usually hidden marketing and design thinking that underpins the ad is reinforced by the panel of copy at the top: "Typo-anarchist Cornel Windlin comes straight outta Zurich with some serious Swiss attitude to wreak havoc on conventional typography wherever he can." This is followed by a list of the materials and technology used by Windlin to create the image.

¶There is something quite poignant about an ad which employs the typographic signifiers of "subversion" to acknowledge its own complicity in the commercial process. But the ad's very knowingness poses larger questions about the purpose, within the commercial arena, of "experimental" or "radical" design. If the aim of the new typographers working within advertising (apart from making some money) is to enlarge the available repertoire of visual languages and shake off the design profession's last few remaining rules and constraints, then the battle appears to have been won.

Aesthetically, almost anything is possible now.

Soft drink can
Design company: Reed Design
Client: Woolworths
Great Britain, 1995

But the question remains: **what exactly, in broader communication terms, is the new typography for?**

Advertisers might reply that the new advertising is open-ended, that viewers are free to pursue their own private associations and make of it what they like. But this apparent openness is merely a means to an end, and this end, not unreasonably, is the same as it ever was: *buy our product.* The Foster's ad tries to achieve it with a double bluff: "Look, we're being 'subversive' and we know you know it's a pose – we're OK." But the only small option for subversion, however original the design, is also the same as it ever was:

savour the aesthetics by all means, but don't buy the product.

¶If radical typography's purpose amounts to nothing more challenging than a new way to shift the goods – and amuse the designer in the process – it is destined to last only as long as it continues to intrigue the consumer. Within the cultural arena, too, experimental typography faces similar pressing questions of purpose. In hard communication terms, leaving aside the deconstructionist theory, which few typographers can be said truly to understand, what is it for? Exciting as it may be to look at, does it represent a functional improvement on more conventional ways of delivering the same essential message? It is easy to justify extreme manipulations of small quantities of text in a poster or a television commercial when the emotion of the message is as important as what the words have to say and, historically, designers have always sought to achieve a balance between typographic legibility and the need for expression.

¶But longer texts for continuous reading pose more demanding problems of interpretation for the typographer. In 30 issues of *Raygun*, David Carson and his design assistants pulled text typography as far from convention as it has ever been taken in a mass-market publication. Carson argued that his intention was to encourage reluctant MTV-generation readers to read, and they wrote to the magazine in droves to say that they liked the approach. Other American designers advanced similar arguments. "Television has conditioned everyone at being very good at discerning what an image is and 'getting' it within a few frames," explained Rick Valicenti. "If you don't like it, you hit the remote control. So print, quite often, does the same thing: it freezes a moment where a lot of things are happening to provide an impression. People can either stay there and engage the interesting aspects, or turn the page."[6]

Spread from *Raygun* no. 14
Designer: Rodney Shelden Fehsenfeld
Art director: David Carson
Client: Ray Gun Publishing
USA, 1994

¶While such claims rapidly became almost axiomatic in some sections of the design world, they remain entirely untested in any rigorous sense of the word. What impact do such typographic strategies have on reading speed and comprehension?

Is it really the case that a text that is typographically demanding to read is more memorable once deciphered?

And how much previous commitment to the subject matter do you need to even want to begin to decipher it?

¶There are certainly many who question the need for designers to intervene so deterministically in the reading process. **Reading, argues British information designer Paul Stiff, is a highly complex, far from passive set of activities, operating on many levels. "When people read," he notes, "they make strategic choices, constantly generating inferences and hypotheses – about intention, relevance, tone of voice, and so on."[7]**

American critic Marc Treib points out that an over-activated text is "like getting a book that is already underlined, and if you have some idiot who is marking phrases that are unimportant in terms of your reading of the book, it's something you have to overcome to get back to the original message."[8] In an issue of the *American Center for Design Journal*, published in 1994, the designers' typographic interpretation of an article, based on footprint shapes, became a source of public bad feeling expressed in a special note tacked on to the article itself by the writers: "As authors, we feel compelled to state our objections to the layout . . . First, we believe that setting the text in the shape of footprints compromises legibility and discourages people from reading . . . Second, while our article compares dancing to interdisciplinary collaboration, dance is a metaphor and not the true subject of the article."[9]

Spread from *American Center for Design Journal* vol. 8 no. 1
Design company: Tanagram
Client: American Center for Design
USA, 1994

Project from *Zed* no. 2
"Selected notes to ZeitGuys"
Designer: Bob Aufuldish
Writer: Mark Bartlett
Client: Virginia Commonwealth University
USA, 1995

¶If a clash such as this, within a journal publicly committed to design as a "form of authorship", suggests there is some way to go before designers and writers routinely coexist in a state of happy interaction, *Typography Now Two* shows that such collaboration can sometimes be achieved. *Emigre*, though it has the self-referential advantage of being a publication about design, continues to offer a model for a typographic articulation of text achieved in a way that is engagingly expressive, genuinely functional and a lasting contribution to practical research. The design journals *Form + Zweck* and *Zed*, publications very much in the *Emigre* tradition, also exhibit a high degree of thoughtfulness in their exploration of the experimental interface of writing and design.

¶In publishing's mainstream, such approaches are still not as common as their academic and advertising impact might lead one to expect, perhaps because the traditional hierarchies and divisions of responsibility are much slower to shift than in small independent publications. *Raygun* aside, *Wired* is perhaps the most striking example of a newsstand publication which attempts to meld typography and image in the service of an editorial vision. *Wired*'s pre-contents introductory pages are "advertisements", inspired by the books of Marshall McLuhan and Quentin Fiore, for key techno-cultural ideas from the heart of the magazine, conceived and realised at journalistic speed in scintillating verbal and visual metaphors for the fluid information transfers of the digital realm.

¶It is too early to say whether the liquid condition of the emerging screen-based typography – see Michael Worthington's *Hypertype* project on page 218 – will have a lasting reciprocal influence on the typography of the paper realm. Print will continue to exist for the foreseeable future, though, and it seems likely that many of the experimental approaches gathered here will become permanent features of typographic practice. More than anything, the picture that emerges from *Typography Now Two* is one of flux and transition. The implosion of traditional typography may, like a sloughed skin, be a sign of renewal, or it may prove to have been a marker of millennial anxiety, profound uncertainty in an accelerating culture, perhaps even long-term decline. That is for future historians to decide. What can be said with some certainty is that the mutations of typography in the 1990s reflect a deep scepticism about received wisdom and a questioning of established authorities, traditional practices and fixed cultural identities, which has parallels throughout society. They tell us a great deal about the increasing value we place, as a culture, in the mediating power of typography as an interpreter of the reality we inhabit. They encapsulate the moment while also, in the largest sense, being wholly of their time.

Spread from *Wired* no. 2.08
Creative director: John Plunkett
Designers: John Plunkett, Eric Adigard
Design company: Plunkett + Kuhr
Client: Wired Ventures
USA, 1994

Subscription card for *Now Time* magazine
Designer: Edward Fella
Client: A.R.T. Press
USA, 1993

1 "Massimo Vignelli vs. Ed Benguiat (sort of)", *Print* XLV:V, September/October 1991.

2 Paul Rand, "From Cassandre to chaos" in *Design, Form and Chaos*, Yale University Press, New Haven and London, 1993.

3 Henry Wolf, "The view of a curmudgeon, junior grade", *AIGA Journal of Graphic Design*, vol. 11 no. 4, 1993.

4 Steven Heller, "Cult of the ugly", *Eye* no. 9 vol. 3, 1993. *Emigre* no. 30, "Fallout", Spring 1994. The "fallout" continued up to the time of writing. In 1996, a digital type foundry, Beaufonts, based in Manchester, England, published a brochure, *Beaufonts 1, Excess Baggage*, containing a text that wittily mangles the words of Heller's original essay to make a perverse kind of (non)sense.

5 Hugh Hart, "It takes all types", *Chicago Tribune*, 2 June 1995.

6 Quoted in Hugh Hart, *Chicago Tribune*.

7 Paul Stiff, "Stop sitting around and start reading", *Eye* no. 11 vol. 3, 1993.

8 Quoted in Michael Dooley, "Kicking up a little dust" in Michael Bierut, William Drenttel, Steven Heller & D. K. Holland (eds.), *Looking Closer: Critical Writings on Graphic Design*, Allworth Press, New York, 1994.

9 Lauralee Alben and Jim Faris, "The interdisciplinary dance (shall we?)", *American Center for Design Journal*, "Interact", vol. 8 no. 1, 1994.

We're page malleable the tech,

trying to nature eerie hand-

to represent of "perfection" made

create its the of imagery

visual opposite: Net. computer- ...

metaphors the We're generated 'high

on a electronic, equally images tech/

static, nonlinear, interested and high

printed infinitely in low- touch".

John Plunkett

SOME READERS MAY CHOOSE TO INTERPRET A LAYOUT AS BEING UNREADABLE; AS HAVING CROSSED THAT LINE BETWEEN FORM AND FUNCTION. THE QUESTION IS: IF WE DIDN'T EXPERIMENT, IF WE SET ALL OUR TYPE IN A THREE COLUMN GRID, WOULD YOU EVEN BE INTERESTED? PROBABLY NOT. THE CLEAN GRID OF MODERNITY HAS BEEN FORMALLY REJECTED BY THE NIHILISM OF INDUSTRIAL YOUTH CULTURE. Joshua Berger

The new ability has become the new aesthetic ... Like the arabesques of the 1880s and the swashes of the 1970s, the contortions of the 1990s will fall out of favour, but not before showing us what the new tools can do.

Tobias Frere-Jones

Massimo Vignelli

commercial

Instead of always looking at it from the point of view that mass consumption is a bad thing, and anything assisting it is guilty by association, perhaps a bit of credit is due to the mainstream for taking some risks, and to the avant-garde for infiltrating mainstream culture ... I'm not saying that the avant-garde exists simply to supply the commercial world with the means to sell more products, but I do think it can be beneficial for both to occasionally share ideologies.

Rudy VanderLans

THE POWER OF CAPITALIST CULTURE TO COMMODIFY AND CONTROL HAS DISPERSED THE DESIGNER'S FORMS AND INSTRUMENTS OF CRITICISM AND MADE THEM HARMLESS IN THE DAZZLING SPECTACLE ...

JAN VAN TOORN

get a good sized cutting board, preferably made out of exquisite wood, like oak or hickory. get your pike, and carefully clean the fish. fillet the fish. preheat the oven to 375 ar carefully place the pike fillets on the cutting board. place in the oven for approximately fiv minutes, or enough to lightly sear the fish. next take a fork and pierce the fillets to determ if they are beginning to get flakey. when cooked to your liking, remove the board from the oven. throw the pike away and eat the board!

recipe for cooking pike

PIKES PEAK LITHOGRAPHING CO

3516 North Tejon Street
Colorado Springs
Colorado 80907
tel 719 632 7276
fax 719 632 0585

ADDRESS CORRECTION REQUESTED

PO BOX 7122
Colorado Springs
Colorado
80933

Classification Esox lucius, family Esocidae.
aka family McLeod
Coloration 4 color except where it is bronze or olive green on the back. Flanks light olive with an overlay of creamy spots and blotches. The fins are red to yellow, the underside white.
Range Throughout Europe, Ireland, the USA and most of northern Europe and parts of North Africa.
Habitat common to Colorado Springs. Normally found in close proximity to paper.
Size can reach a length of 77 inches can reach a width of 54.5 inches

we're talking...

LARGE sheet 54.5

2"   6"   1'

Promotional poster for a large-sheet printer
DESIGNER/ILLUSTRATOR April Greiman
PRINCIPAL TYPEFACES Baskerville, DIN Mittelschrift, OCRA, Bell Gothic
CLIENT Pikes Peak Lithographing

USA, 1994

Better call Scott. I think we got a big one!

since 1949 PIKES PEAK LITHOGRAPHING CO

inches

Perfectly adapted for a life of murder and may-
hem, the pike blends in with beds of water weed. The fins and tail
are **large**, giving the fish **rapid acceleration**
as and when required. The head of the pike is flattened and the large
eyes are set high up in the skull. It's jaws are large, **strong**
and bony. The teeth are long and pointed and there is a ridge of
sharp but small teeth on the roof of the fish's mouth. Lazy by incli-
nation, pike are **often happy** to scavenge on dead food.
They are also **active and effective** hunters,
more than capable of catching fish of up to half
their own body weight.

5' 5"or 65"

76"

77"

65"

54.5"

High-speed dubbing *on double well boom boxes puts additional stress on a tape's performance and on the cassette mechanism.*

The long wavelengths of the bass can suffer without a cassette mechanism that:

● minimizes tape skew

● promotes good head contact

● provides smooth, consistent tape motion at high speed.

TDK DS-X'S TAPE AND CASSETTE MECHANISM HAS BEEN ENGINEERED FOR 2X HIGH-SPEED DUBBING. TDK'S EXPERIENCE IN DUPLICATING, AT SPEEDS OF 64X AND MORE, LAID THE FOUNDATION. BUILT SOLID TO SURVIVE DUB AFTER DUB.

5

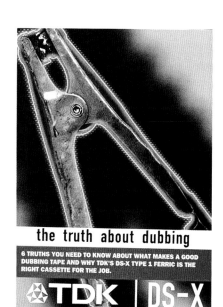

the truth about dubbing

6 TRUTHS YOU NEED TO KNOW ABOUT WHAT MAKES A GOOD DUBBING TAPE AND WHY TDK'S DS-X TYPE 1 FERRIC IS THE RIGHT CASSETTE FOR THE JOB.

◈TDK | DS-X

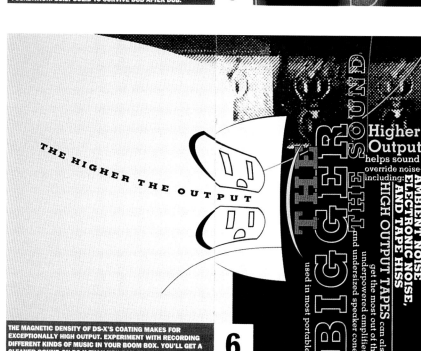

THE HIGHER THE OUTPUT

Higher Output helps sound override noise-including:

AMBIENT NOISE, ELECTRONIC NOISE, AND TAPE HISS.

HIGH OUTPUT TAPES can also get the most out of the underpowered amplifiers and undersized speaker cones used in most portables

THE BIGGER THE SOUND

THE MAGNETIC DENSITY OF DS-X'S COATING MAKES FOR EXCEPTIONALLY HIGH OUTPUT. EXPERIMENT WITH RECORDING DIFFERENT KINDS OF MUSIC IN YOUR BOOM BOX. YOU'LL GET A CLEANER SOUND ON DS-X THAN YOU CAN ON ANY OTHER FERRIC.

6

The Truth Series

Promotional mailers

ART DIRECTOR / Steve Farrar

DESIGNERS / Kirk James, Andrew Szurley, Richard Curren

DESIGN COMPANY / Jager Di Paola Kemp Design

PRINCIPAL TYPEFACES / Franklin Gothic, DIN

CLIENT / TDK

USA, 1993-94

Team TDK is a progamme developed to deliver product information, services and merchandising tools to the sales forces of music and audio stores. Each of the three mailers contained a blank cassette and a cassette-sized educational booklet aimed at design-aware retail managers and sales people. By keeping copy short and direct and reinforcing it with dynamic conceptual imagery, the designers hoped to make information easier to absorb and recall.

this is a world full of noise.

noise destroys sound quality. noises, *such as hiss*, are inherent to all magnetic tape recordings. the better the tape, the lower the hiss

THERE IS ABOUT 1000 TIMES MORE NOISE IN AN LP THAN IN A CD. TDK SA-X IS THE QUIETEST TAPE ON THE PLANET - PERFECT FOR RECORDING CD'S.

1

signal-to-noise ratio the tape noise spec you see most often

measures how faint inherent tape noise is. the bigger the number the fainter the noise. that's it. simple.

TDK PIONEERED THE DUAL-LAYER MAGNETIC COATING USED IN SA-X. TREBLE AND BASS EACH HAVE THEIR OWN CUSTOMIZED COATING LAYER, ACHIEVING THE HIGHEST SIGNAL-TO-NOISE RATIO ON THE MARKET.

2

magnetise

IT TAKES HIGHER POWER TO MAGNETIZE THE COBALT IN SA

*POWER EQUALS BIAS

THAT'S WHY IT'S CALLED A HIGH-BIAS TAPE THE EXTRA POWER OF A HIGH-BIAS TAPE PAYS OFF IN BETTER FREQUENCY RESPONSE, HIGHER OUTPUT AND LESS NOISE.

BECAUSE OF ITS HOT HIGH END, HIGH-BIAS TDK SA HAS HALF THE HISS LEVELS OF NORMAL-BIAS TAPES.

1

sa's micro engineered cassette

not only keeps tape motion precise but it stands up to kicking around in the car

AND SA'S GREAT HIGH-FREQUENCY PERFORMANCE IS IMPORTANT FOR CAR STEREOS BECAUSE ROAD AND WIND NOISE OFTEN DROWN OUT THE HIGHS ON TYPICAL TAPES. SO REV IT UP IF YOU STICK TO SA.

TRY THIS IN A VERY NOISY CAR: PLAY YOUR DOLBY TAPES WITH THE DOLBY SWITCHED OFF. THE HIGHS GET BOOSTED AND ARE EASIER TO HEAR. EXPERIMENT WITH TDK SA.

4

Electronic Telegraph

Information sheet for online newspaper
DESIGNER Carlo Tartaglia
PRINCIPAL TYPEFACE Helvetica
CLIENT The Telegraph

Great Britain, 1995

Punctvox

Graphic stings for a German news channel
DESIGNERS Andy Altmann, David Ellis
DESIGN COMPANY Why Not Associates
PHOTOGRAPHER Rocco Redondo
PRINCIPAL TYPEFACE Template Gothic
CLIENT Vox TV

Great Britain, 1994

In 1985, **VTR** was established as a new kind of **VIDEO FACILITIES HOUSE** – one where technical excellence would go hand in hand with friendly, professional client care.

concept

WE WERE A SMALL COMPANY THEN, BUT OUR AMBITIONS WERE BIG: we invested in the best equipment and recruited the most talented operators in town. Word spread within the industry, and soon we had built up a broad and loyal client base. And we haven't stopped growing ever since.

We are now one of London's TOP post-production houses, employing more than 80 staff.

We also have two sister companies whose resources complement our own:
THE MACHINE ROOM TAPE-TO-TAPE CONVERSION AND DUPLICATION
BLUE BROADCAST POST-PRODUCTION

Although we've expanded, the **VTR** philosophy remains the same: we believe that technical wizardry is only part of the picture – teamwork is what makes us succeed.

Promotional brochure for a TV and video facilities house
DESIGNERS Andy Altmann, David Ellis, Patrick Morrissey
DESIGN COMPANY Why Not Associates
PHOTOGRAPHERS Photonica, PhotoDisc
PRINCIPAL TYPEFACE Meta
CLIENT VTR

Great Britain, 1995

We want every job to be as **worry-free** AS POSSIBLE, FROM **concept** meeting right through to completion.

THAT'S WHERE THE **VTR** PRODUCTION TEAM COMES IN: they are there to **provide clients with** PROFESSIONAL ADVICE and friendly support from start

WE ALSO HAVE A TRAINED ENGINEERING DEPARTMENT ON HAND AT ALL TIMES TO ENSURE THE smooth RUNNING OF OUR EQUIPMENT.

AXIAL D.C.P.
MATADOR SGI EXTREMES HENRY
ALIAS URSA GOLD
IMAGE 3D **PARALLAX ADVANCE**

With a broad range of the best equipment there is — including Henrys, Ursa Gold telecines, Axial edit suites, Parallax Advance, Alias and Softimage 3D—we can find the solution for even the most demanding project, whether it's multi-layering, morphing or any other special effect. But although we're at the forefront of technological innovation, we put the emphasis firmly on user-friendliness: we want to dazzle you with the results, not blind you with science.

equipment

ANITA RODDICK•IVAN ILLICH•PAUL HAWKEN•HERMAN DALY•SUSAN GRIFFIN
VACLAV HAVEL•LISA CARVER•TERRY TEMPEST WILLIAMS•BOBBY MCFERRIN

UTNE UR READER

JAN-FEB 95   NO. 67 | THE BEST OF THE ALTERNATIVE MEDIA | $4.95 USA $5.95 CAN

VISIONARIES 100
WHO
COULD CHANGE
YOUR
LIFE

01
7 25274 73926 4

BELL HOOKS • CONSERVATIVES AGAINST GINGRICH • LESLIE SAVAN • RICHARD
RODRIGUEZ • BEN CHAVIS • SOUTH AFRICA • QUEEN ITCHIE • THE BODY AS MUSIC

UTNE UR READER

MARCH-APRIL 95   NO.68 | THE BEST OF THE ALTERNATIVE MEDIA | $4.95 USA $5.95 CAN

CYBERHOOD VS NEIGHBORHOOD

Are computer networks
real communities?
(Are neighborhoods?)

03
7 25274 73926 4

Utne Reader no. 67

Magazine cover

DESIGNER DIRECTORS	Jan Jancourt, Andrew Henderson
ASSOCIATE ART DIRECTOR	Andrew Henderson
DESIGN COMPANY	Jancourt & Associates
PRINCIPAL TYPEFACE	Officina
CLIENT	LENS Publishing

USA, 1995

Utne Reader no. 68

Magazine cover and spreads

DESIGN DIRECTORS	Jan Jancourt, Andrew Henderson
ASSOCIATE ART DIRECTOR	Andrew Henderson
DESIGN COMPANY	Jancourt & Associates
PRINCIPAL TYPEFACE	Officina
CLIENT	LENS Publishing

USA, 1995

Utne Reader is an independently published
digest of new writing and articles of
interest selected from other publications,
both marginal and mainstream. In 1994,
eleven years after it was founded by Eric
Utne, the magazine's editorial philosophy
was rethought and a redesign was
commissioned to embody its new vision. The
Reader's new format is both livelier than
before and more rigorous in mood, while
transmitting the urgency of its socially and
culturally attuned content.

CYBERHOOD VS NEIGHBORHOOD

Is There a There in Cyberspace?

SPECIAL TO UTNE READER | John Perry Barlow

I am often asked how I went from pushing cows around a remote Wyoming ranch to my present occupation (which *Wall Street Journal* recently described as "cyberspace cadet"). I haven't got a short answer, but I suppose I came to the virtual world looking for community.

Unlike most modern Americans, I grew up in an actual place, an entirely nonintentional community called Pinedale, Wyoming. As I struggled for nearly a generation to keep my ranch in the family, I was motivated by the belief that such places were the spiritual home of humanity. But I knew their future was not promising.

At the dawn of the 20th century, over 40 percent of the American workforce lived off the land. The majority of us lived in towns like Pinedale. Now fewer than 1 percent of us extract a living from the soil. We just became too productive for our own good.

Of course, the population followed the jobs. Farming and ranching communities are now home to a demographically insignificant percentage of Americans, the vast majority of whom live not in ranch houses but in more or less identical split-level "ranch homes" in more or less identical suburban "communities." Generica.

In my view, these are neither communities nor homes. I believe the combination of television and suburban population patterns is simply toxic to the soul. I see much evidence in contemporary America to support this view.

Meanwhile, back at the ranch, doom impended. And, as I watched community in Pinedale growing ill from the same economic forces that were killing my family's ranch, the Bar Cross, satellite dishes brought the cultural infection of television. I started looking around for evidence that community in America would not perish altogether.

I took some heart in the mysterious nomadic City of the Deadheads, the virtually physical town that follows the Grateful Dead around the country. The Deadheads lacked place, touching down briefly wherever the band happened to be playing, and they lacked continuity in time, since they had to suffer a new diaspora every time the band moved on or went home. But they had many of the other necessary elements of community, including a culture, a religion of sorts (which, though it lacked dogma, had most of the other, more nurturing aspects of spiritual practice), a sense of necessity, and, most importantly, shared adversity.

I wanted to know more about the flavor of their interaction, what they thought and felt, but since I wrote Dead songs (including "Estimated Prophet" and "Cassidy"), I was a minor icon to the Deadheads, and was thus inhibited, in some socially Heisenbergian way, from getting a clear view of what really went on among them.

Then, in 1987, I heard about a "place" where Deadheads gathered where I could move among them without distorting too much the field of observation. Better, this was a place I could visit without leaving Wyoming. It was a shared computer in Sausalito, California, called the Whole Earth 'Lectronic Link, or WELL. After a lot of struggling with modems, serial cables, init strings, and other computer arcana that seemed utterly out of phase with such notions as Deadheads and small towns, I found myself looking at the glowing yellow word "Login:" beyond which lay my future.

"Inside" the WELL, were Deadheads in community. There were thousands of them there, gossiping, complaining (mostly about the Grateful Dead), comforting and harassing each other, bartering, engaging in religion (or at least exchanging their totemic set lists), beginning and ending love affairs, praying for one another's sick kids. There was, it seemed, everything one might find going on in a small town, save dragging Main Street and making out on the back roads.

I was delighted. I felt I had found the new locale of

> *Computer networking can help bring community
  back to the center of modern life*

CYBERHOOD VS NEIGHBORHOOD

The Virtual Community

Howard Rheingold

In the summer of 1986, my then-2-year-old daughter picked up a tick. There was this blood-bloated *thing* sucking on our baby's scalp, and we weren't quite sure how to go about getting it off. My wife, Judy, called the pediatrician. It was 11 o'clock in the evening. I logged onto the WELL, the big Bay Area infonet, and contacted the Parenting conference (a conference is an on-line conversation about a specific subject). I got my answer on-line within minutes from a fellow with the improbable but genuine name of Flash Gordon, M.D. I had removed the tick by the time Judy got the callback from the pediatrician's office.

What amazed me wasn't just the speed with which we obtained precisely the information we needed to know, right when we needed to know it. It was also the immense inner sense of security that comes with discovering that real people—most of them parents, some of them nurses, doctors, and midwives—are available, around the clock, if you need them. There is a magic protective circle around the atmosphere of the Parenting conference. We're talking about our sons and daughters in this forum, not about our computers or our opinions about philosophy, and many of us feel that this tacit understanding sanctifies the virtual space.

The atmosphere of this particular conference—the attitudes people exhibit to each other in the tone of what they say in public—is part of what continues to attract me. People who never have much to contribute in political debate, technical argument, or intellectual gamesmanship turn out to have a lot to say about raising children. People you knew as fierce, even nasty, intellectual opponents in other contexts gave you emotional support on a deeper level, parent to parent, within the boundaries of this small but warmly human corner of cyberspace.

In most cases, people who talk about a shared interest don't disclose enough about themselves as whole individuals on-line to inspire real trust in others. But in the case of the subcommunity called the Parenting conference, a few dozen of us, scattered across the country, few of whom rarely if ever saw the others face to face, have a few years of minor crises to knit us together and prepare us for serious business when it comes our way. Another several dozen read the conference regularly but contribute only when they have something important to add. Hundreds more read the conference every week without comment, except when something extraordinary happens.

Jay Allison and his family live in Massachusetts. He and his wife are public-radio producers. I've never met them face to face, although I feel I know something powerful and intimate about the Allisons and have strong emotional ties to them. What follows are some of Jay's postings on the WELL:

"Woods Hole. Midnight. I am sitting in the dark of my daughter's room. Her monitor lights blink at me. The lights used to blink too brightly so I covered them with bits of bandage adhesive and now they flash faintly underneath, a persistent red and green, Lillie's heart and lungs.

"Above the monitor is her portable suction unit. In the glow of the flashlight I'm writing by, it looks like the plastic guts of a science-class human model, the tubes coiled around the power supply; the reservoir, the pump.

"Tina is upstairs trying to get some sleep. A baby monitor links our bedroom to Lillie's. It links our sleep to Lillie's too, and because our souls are linked to hers, we do not sleep well.

"I am naked. My stomach is full of beer. The flashlight rests on it, and the beam rises and falls with my breath. My daughter breathes through a white plastic tube inserted into a hole in her throat. She's 14 months old."

Sitting in front of our computers with our hearts racing and tears in our eyes, in Tokyo and Sacramento and Austin, we read about Lillie's croup, her tracheostomy, the

autumn winter

cakewalk

95

®
cakewalk

28

Double-sided point-of-sale promotion
for a children's clothing manufacturer
DESIGNERS / Andy Altmann, David Ellis, Patrick Morrissey
DESIGN COMPANY / Why Not Associates
PRINCIPAL TYPEFACE / Template Gothic
CLIENT / Cakewalk

Great Britain, 1995

Lotus: This is Notes

Television commercial

DIRECTOR | Jeffrey Plansker
ART DIRECTOR | Steve Sumne
DESIGN DIRECTOR | P. Scott Makela
DESIGN COMPANY | Words and Pictures for Business and Culture
SPECIAL PHOTOGRAPHY | Laura Plansker
PRINCIPAL TYPEFACES | Dead History, Barmeno
CLIENT | Lotus Software Corporation

USA, 1994

Everything + Nothing

Audio CD cover for David Sylvian
DESIGNER | P. Scott Makela
DESIGN COMPANY | Words and Pictures for Business and Culture
PHOTOGRAPHER | Billy Phelps
PRINCIPAL TYPEFACE | WAC Mittelschrift
CLIENT | Virgin Records

USA, 1994

The Rescinded Muse

Poster/brochure for a paper company

DESIGNERS	Allen Hori, Charlie Becker, Rob Eberhardt
DESIGN COMPANY	Bates Hori
WRITER	Augustine Hope
PHOTOGRAPHERS	Gaye Chan, Allen Hori
PRINCIPAL TYPEFACES	Helvetica, News Gothic, Bell Gothic
CLIENT	Potlatch Corporation

USA, 1994

Allen Hori's paper promotion is a complex "ode to music" which equates the poetic discoveries of the design process with the intuitive explorations of music-making. The recycled paper's character is reflected in the way the press sheet is structured to eliminate trimming and unnecessary wastage. The viewer can treat the piece as a double-sided poster, or use its perforations to take it apart and reassemble it as a brochure.

Wired's pre-contents introductory pages are a rare example of structural innovation within a commercial newsstand magazine. Each issue, a quotation from a main editorial feature embodying a key cultural or technological idea becomes the designers' starting point for a McLuhanesque four-page visual essay. Often the typography is woven into the image so tightly that the two become almost indivisible – a new style of journalistic communication that is simultaneously both highly suggestive and editorially specific.

"The medium,

or process, of our time – electric technology – is reshaping and restructuring patterns of social interdependence and every aspect of our personal life.

It is forcing us to reconsider and re-evaluate practically Everything is changing....................

every thought, every action, and every institution

formerly taken for granted.

you,

what happens *when you combine media voyeurism, technological exhibitionism, and strategic simulations?*

your education,

your government,

your family,

your neighborhood,

And they're using

your relation to the others."

your job,

Wired no. 1.1

Magazine spreads
CREATIVE DIRECTOR	John Plunkett
DESIGNERS	John Plunkett,
	Eric Adigard
DESIGN COMPANY	Plunkett + Kuhr
ILLUSTRATOR	Eric Adigard
PRINCIPAL TYPEFACE	Myriad
CLIENT	Wired USA

USA, 1993

news flash:

in the 21st century army you get the

cyber-deterrent

Wired no. 2.09

Magazine spreads
CREATIVE DIRECTOR	John Plunkett
DESIGNERS	John Plunkett,
	Thomas Schneider
DESIGN COMPANY	Plunkett + Kuhr
ILLUSTRATOR	Eric Adigard
PRINCIPAL TYPEFACE	Myriad
CLIENT	Wired Ventures

USA, 1994

Wired no. 3.02

CREATIVE DIRECTORS | John Plunkett,
Barbara Kuhr
DESIGNERS | Thomas Schneider,
Johan Vipper
PRINCIPAL TYPEFACE | Helvetica
CLIENT | Wired Ventures

USA, 1995

Magazine spreads

Wired no. 3.08

CREATIVE DIRECTORS | John Plunkett,
Barbara Kuhr
DESIGNERS | John Plunkett,
Thomas Schneider,
Eric Adigard
ILLUSTRATOR | Eric Adigard
PRINCIPAL TYPEFACE | Akzidenz Grotesk
CLIENT | Wired Ventures

USA, 1995

Magazine spreads

"Remember my name," the virus says, which after all is just another way of saying, "I'm alive."

Julian Dibbell, page 126

(as a cultural force, it's a dead end.)

— John Brockman, page 118

The Future's Paper

Print campaign
WRITERS/DESIGNERS   Rick Valicenti, Su McLoughlin, Mark Rattlin
DIGITAL IMAGING   Rick Valicenti, Mark Rattlin
DESIGN COMPANY   Thirst
PHOTOGRAPHER   William Valicenti
PRINCIPAL TYPEFACE   Cyberotica
CLIENT   Gilbert Paper

USA, 1994

"The Future's Paper" print campaign authored by Thirst consisted of two trilogies and each of the double-page ads ran just once in *Wired*. For the more "human" second series, "Realize Change", familiar iconography – Clark Kent, Betty Crocker, Elvis – was futuristically recast. In a non-typographic extension of the project, Rick Valicenti's photographer brother took life-sized enlargements of the figures to a Midwestern shopping mall, where he invited shoppers to pose with their preferred character – a "twisted look", Valicenti claims, at contemporary confusions between fantasy and reality.

Das ist der Air Elite Structure, oder kurz **Der Schuh.**

Der Schuh zum **WIRBELN, SPRINGEN** und **TANZEN** für stundenlange Aerobic-Hochstimmung.

Der Schuh mit dem **Flexile Air System,** das den Vorfuß bei jeder Beugung dämpft.

Der Schuh, der so leuchtend weiß ist, daß er Dir für die Straße viel zu schade ist.

Der Schuh mit Dämpfung im Fersenbereich.

Der Schuh mit dem bequemen, gepolsterten Knöchelkragen.

Der Schuh, der so anmutig aussieht. **Der Schuh** mit dem schnittigen Nike® Logo.

Der Schuh, der eine Sie ist. Die Schuh.

Just do it!

NIKE AIR

Nike: The Shoe

Print campaign
DESIGNERS / Chris Priest, Andy Altmann, David Ellis
DESIGN COMPANY / Why Not Associates
AGENCY / Wieden Kennedy
PHOTOGRAPHER / Hans Pieterse
PRINCIPAL TYPEFACE / Franklin Gothic
CLIENT / Nike

Great Britain, 1992

Tant qu'il y aura des dunks

Poster/brochure to promote a five-on-five basketball tournam
DESIGNER / Robert Nakata
AGENCY / Wieden & Kennedy
WRITER / Ernest Lupinacci
PHOTOGRAPHER / Hans Pieterse
PRINCIPAL TYPEFACE / Monaco
CLIENT / Nike France

The Netherlands, 1994

Le
Nike 5 x 5

5 x 5 Tant qu'il y aura des dunk

Le tournoi de basket

24-25 sept.,
Parc Départemental
de Bron-Parilly,
15 rue du Clos Verger,
Vennissieux;

Le tournoi de basket 5x5 de Nike
débarque à Lyon, samedi 24 septembre.
Améne tes baskets et tes 36 cm de
détente séche au parc départemental de
Bron-Parilly - 15 rue du Clos Verger à
Vénnissieux - à 13 heures tapantes et
Nike te mettra dans une équipe avec 4
autres joueurs.
Reste dans le coin et reviens dimanche
à 11 heures. Ce sera la derniére phase
de qualification, avant la finale à
Paris, du Raid Outdoor 3x3 de Nike.
2 supers tournois de basket pour le
dernier week-end de l'été...t'es gâté!

Au coucher du soleil, quand les derniers
sifflets se seront tus et que le panier
aura fini de trembler, nous saurons qui
est vraiment le numéro 1.
Le tournoi est gratuit et ouvert à tous.
Alors fonce chez INTERSPORT ou MAG SPORT
pour t'inscrire avant le 22 septembre.

Pour te rendre au tournoi:
En voiture: prends le périphérique,
sors à Saint-Priest Centre et au 1er feu,
à gauche. En métro: prends la ligne D et
descends à la station Parilly.

The new Air Trainer Max²™ →

shoe's dual air pressure technology matches the movement and impact of the foot.

Ken Griffey, Jr., baseball player, wears the Air Trainer Max² cross-training shoe from Nike.

In running, the heel strikes first, so 5 psi (at inflation), lower density air is located in the center of the heel Air-Sole® unit. This "softer" air provides maximum cushioning after jumps. Higher density, 25 psi (at inflation), air wraps around the heel for firmness and stability. The "air" used is usually a gas that won't deflate over the lifetime of the shoe.

A forefoot Air-Sole® unit gives extra cushioning.

What is technology but mind pushing the limits of muscle

NIKE

Air Max 2 Technical

Print campaign

DESIGNER Robert Nakata
AGENCY Wieden & Kennedy
WRITER Jean Rhode
PHOTOGRAPHER Hans Pieterse (shoes)
PRINCIPAL TYPEFACE Corporate S
CLIENT Nike USA

The Netherlands, 1994

Nike Running

	Print campaign
DESIGNER	Robert Nakata
AGENCY	Wieden & Kennedy
WRITER	Evelyn Monroe
PRINCIPAL TYPEFACE	DIN Mittelschrift
CLIENT	Nike Europe

The Netherlands, 1994

Nike Running

	Print campaign
DESIGNER	Robert Nakata
AGENCY	Wieden & Kennedy
WRITERS	Ernest Lupinacci, Giles Montgomery, Bob Moore
PHOTOGRAPHER	John Huet
PRINCIPAL TYPEFACES	Argos, DIN Mittelschrift
CLIENT	Nike Europe

The Netherlands, 1995

Rock stars

and CEO's are starting to dress alike. There is a
revolution
going on.
The walls are coming down.
The best artists are businesspeople.
The best businesspeople are artists.

If you do not love
your job,
change it.
Instead of
pushing paper,
push ideas.
Instead of sitting down,
stand up and be heard. contribute.
Instead of complaining,
Don't get stuck
in a job description.

Microsoft Office

Print campaign
DESIGNER | Robert Nakata
AGENCY | Wieden & Kennedy
WRITER | Bob Moore
PHOTOGRAPHER | Dieter Eikelpoth
PRINCIPAL TYPEFACE | Corporate S
CLIENT | Microsoft

The Netherlands, 1994-95

Each of the three portraits – rock star, businessman, young boy – is followed by an "image" spread and, through the copy's emphasis and lack of visible computer, it is hoped the viewer will understand that Microsoft makes software and not hardware. The typography suggests the ease and fluidity with which information can be manipulated in the digital realm, as well as its personal dimension, without resorting to an obviously "computer" look in the choice of typeface.

Altmann's Tongue

Book jacket
DESIGNER   Barbara De Wilde
DESIGN COMPANY   De Wilde Design
PRINCIPAL TYPEFACE Brodovitch Albro
CLIENT   Knopf

USA, 1994

The Unusual Life of Tristan Smith

Book jacket
DESIGNER / Chip Kidd
DESIGN COMPANY / Chip Kidd Design
PRINCIPAL TYPEFACE / Univers
CLIENT / Knopf

USA, 1994

The Information

Book jacket
DESIGNER | Chip Kidd
DESIGN COMPANY | Chip Kidd Design
PRINCIPAL TYPEFACE | Bulmer
CLIENT | Harmony Books

USA, 1995

Cowgirl

Promotional poster for a single by Underworld

DESIGNER | John Warwicker
DESIGN COMPANY | Tomato
PRINCIPAL TYPEFACES | Custom-made for the project
CLIENT | Junior Boys Own

Great Britain, 1994

underw orld : born s lippy .   ,

underw orld : born s lippy .TEL EMATIC ; cowg irl; (W INJER MIX .)

a side, born slippy; TELEMATIC. b side, cowgirl (WINJER MIX). written/produced/mixed by UNDERWORLD (smith/hyde/emerson). ℗ + © junior boys own, 1995. junior recordings ltd, the saga centre, 326 kensal road, london w10 5bz, tel 0181 960 4495, fax 0181 960 3256. published by underworld/sherlock holmes music. management: jukes productions, tel 0171 286 9532. manufactured and distributed by rtm/pinnacle. made in england.

jbo29R   JUNIOR BOY'S OWN   5 026734 002900

Born Slippy

Record sleeve for a 12-inch single by Un
DESIGNERS   Jason Kedgley, Graham Wood
DESIGN COMPANY   Tomato
PRINCIPAL TYPEFACE   Bureau Grotesque
CLIENT   Junior Boys Own

Great Britain, 1995

Revolution Radio

Television commercial
DIRECTOR | Walter Pitt
ANIMATOR/EDITOR/PHOTOGRAPHER | Alexei Tylevich
PRINCIPAL TYPEFACES | Custom-made for the project
CLIENT | Rev 105

USA, 1994

Revolution Radio, an alternative music
station based in Minneapolis, gave Alexei
Tylevich complete freedom in his choice
of imagery and use of editing for a
TV commercial. Tylevich's animation
was one of a number of segments
assigned to different designers.
The segments were then spliced
together in a televisual version
of Exquisite Corpse, the Surrealist
game in which each player contributes
a section of a drawing without seeing
what the other players have drawn.

the "end of print" bible of music + style

R AYGUN,

soundgarden
tool
elvis
seaweed
brand new heavies
table of contents
masthead
letters
sound imprint

april'94
$3.50 usa
$3.95 can.

Raygun no. 15

Magazine cover
ART DIRECTOR/DESIGNER David Carson
PHOTOGRAPHERS Davies and Starr
CLIENT Ray Gun Publishing

USA, 1994

Raygun no. 5

Magazine cover
ART DIRECTOR/DESIGNER | David Carson
ILLUSTRATOR | Jim Sherraden
PHOTOGRAPHER | Merlyn Rosenberg
CLIENT | Ray Gun Publishing

USA, 1993

Raygun no. 19

Magazine cover
ART DIRECTOR/DESIGNER | David Carson
PHOTOGRAPHER | Colin Bell
PRINCIPAL TYPEFACE | Teenager
CLIENT | Ray Gun Publishing

USA, 1994

Raygun no. 31

Magazine cover
ART DIRECTORS/DESIGNERS | Hal Wolverton, Alicia Johnson
DESIGN COMPANY | Johnson & Wolverton
PHOTOGRAPHER | Doug Aitken
PRINCIPAL TYPEFACE | Interstate
CLIENT | Ray Gun Publishing

USA, 1995

Raygun no. 27

Magazine cover
ART DIRECTION/DESIGNER | David Carson
PHOTOGRAPHER | David Stewart
PRINCIPAL TYPEFACE | Neulin Sans
CLIENT | Ray Gun Publishing

USA, 1995

Raygun no. 19

Magazine spread
ART DIRECTOR/DESIGNER   David Carson
ILLUSTRATOR   Christian Northeast
PRINCIPAL TYPEFACE   Teenager
CLIENT   Ray Gun Publishing

USA, 1994

Raygun no. 14

Magazine spread
ART DIRECTOR/DESIGNER   David Carson
PHOTOGRAPHER   Chris Cuffaro
CLIENT   Ray Gun Publishing

USA, 1994

Raygun no. 15

Magazine spread
ART DIRECTOR/DESIGNER David Carson
ILLUSTRATOR Malcolm Tarlofsky
CLIENT Ray Gun Publishing

USA, 1994

Raygun no. 18

Magazine spread
ART DIRECTOR/DESIGNER David Carson
PHOTOGRAPHER Allen Messer
CLIENT Ray Gun Publishing

USA, 1994

Raygun no. 19

Magazine Spreads

ART DIRECTOR David Carson
DESIGNER Martin Venezky
CLIENT Ray Gun Publishing

USA, 1994

Raygun no. 29

Magazine spread
ART DIRECTOR/DESIGNER David Carson
ILLUSTRATORS Vera Daucher,
Sarah Cromwell,
Nick Whiting
PRINCIPAL TYPEFACE Neulin Sans
CLIENT Ray Gun Publishing

USA, 1995

RootDOWN

the essence

of DUB

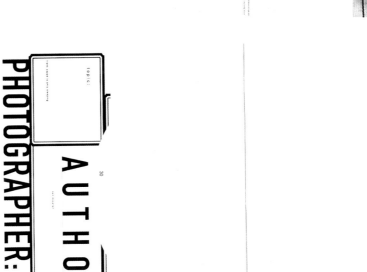

by Aidin Vaziri

Dub is the sound of the new frontier. All spacey echoes and reverberating rhythms it has quietly endured through generations of pop music and consistently slinked its way into the consciousness of cutting-edge artists. It's a style whose threads can be traced in everything from ragga swagger to ambient-driven grooves to unadulterated pop excessiveness. Without barriers or a defining genre, it has quickly become the most versatile and recognizable form of Jamaican music outside of its organic shell. And while many underground flavors of the week — anyone remember acid house, hardcore techno or rare groove? — have come and gone, dub remains strong.

Now more than ever, dub is making its imprint on the works of popular artists. With the recent success of the collaborative Massive Attack and Mad Professor remix album, the rise of UK musicians bred on a steady diet of John Peel's influential radio program and a label boom within the industry, dub is witnessing a high profile largely considered impossible for such an unassuming style. But predictions be damned. Its nucleus has not only gone on to dominate the booming trip-hop scene but continues to blossom in the most unlikely of outlets. Eugan's latest endeavor is laden with certain dub fundamentals, while K Records guru Calvin Johnson has gone under the guise of Dub Narcotic Sound System to turn out some impressively rootsy material, including a remix for the Jon Spencer Blues Explosion.

Since its inception, dub has produced a handful of reliable colonists, such as Adrian Sherwood, African Head Charge, Augustus Pablo, Bill Laswell, Dub Syndicate, Mad Professor, King Jammy, King Tubby, Lee Scratch Perry, Prince Far I, Sly Dunbar & Robbie Shakespeare, Scientist and Zion Train; a batch of dependable labels has also cropped up. On U Sound, Ariwa Universal Egg, Roir, Mo' Wax and RAS. But aside from the original rêkta flavor, the genre has made a vast impact on electronic music: generating a bevy of heavy echoes, mid-tempos and studio trickery on several ambient and techno releases. most notably those at high-profile artists like the Orb, Leftfield and Orbital. There's been considerable pop seepage, too, as witnessed on Primal Scream's 'Higher Than The Sun' and the Boo Radley's 'Lazarus.' All of which suggests that dub is currently the most sought-after ingredient by audio risk-takers.

Dub has had a huge influence on house music in its broadest sense — the breakdowns, drops, drum and bass loops, mad noises, vocal and spoken samples and so on,' says Richard Whittingham of Rockers Hi-Fi, whose latest release Rockers To Rockers seamlessly fuses many of these fundamentals with futuristic dance music. 'The space, the bass and the noises and the way bits of the original track peek out from behind a wall of echo every now and then. But what sets dub apart from a lot of modern music is its spirit and soul which cannot be manufactured to make commercial hits. We don't think of ourselves as a dub band or whatever. Dub is something that milumeen our sound along with loads of other styles. We're just making original music.

Skip McDonald, who forever changed the course of dub music with Tackhead and continues to do so with his new outlet Little Axe, shares a similar perspective. 'There's no dabbling with dub,' he says. 'What I try to do is combine the spirit of the past by mixing blues and dub together. Dub lits in with all about it.'

ART DIRECTOR/DESIGNER David Carson
PHOTOGRAPHER Aldo Mauro
CLIENT Ray Gun Publishing

USA, 1995

Raygun no. 30

Magazine spread

In the issues leading up to David Carson's departure from *Raygun*, there was already evidence of a move towards a much quieter typography described by the magazine's publisher, Marvin Scott Jarrett, as "a new simplicity". This was most starkly apparent in issue 30, Carson's swansong, where in place of his customary fractured headline treatments he devised a label-like credit box that emphasised the contributors' functions rather than their bylines.

Bikini no. 3

Magazine spread
DESIGN DIRECTOR | Scott Clum
DESIGN COMPANY | Ride Design
PHOTOGRAPHER | Cynthia Levine
ILLUSTRATOR | Scott Clum
PRINCIPAL TYPEFACES | Matrix, Osprey
CLIENT | Ray Gun Publishing

USA, 1994

Bikini no. 11

Magazine spread
DESIGN DIRECTOR | Scott Clum
DESIGN COMPANY | Ride Design
PHOTOGRAPHER | Cole Coonce
PRINCIPAL TYPEFACE | Blur
CLIENT | Ray Gun Publishing

USA, 1995

Now is the future and the future is electro-harmonic ...men at play and men at work will meld into one electro-magnetic meeting ... the life-force of genetic interactivity is shackled by the toggle of a cosmic electron-plot. In ether-watery audiate here's B++X tune into the crystal ball of electronic telepresence, activity and media for your mind.

58

59

Bikini no. 2

Magazine spread
DESIGN DIRECTOR   Scott Clum
DESIGNERS   Rey International
DESIGN COMPANY   Ride Design
CLIENT   Ray Gun Publishing

THE YOUNG AMERICANS

photoGraphy by
MELODIE MCDANIEL

StYLing by
RACHEL SAGE

welcome to the
CHELSEA
HOTEL
Legend
precedes
the
Chelsea
Hotel.
by N. Hollis Brown

The gold-colored, important plaques marking either side of the building's entrance honor the fact that both Dylan Thomas and Arthur Miller once made the hotel their homes—Thomas lapsed into a fatal coma in Room 205. Warhol filmed many of his early avant-garde films there, including *The Chelsea Girls*. Leonard Cohen exalted Janis Joplin in his song, "Chelsea Hotel #2." The 1978 stabbing of Nancy Spungen by Sex Pistol Sid Vicious was immortalized in the film *Sid and Nancy*. And the list goes on.

The Chelsea Hotel, 222 West 23rd Street, is literally a historic landmark, officially designated to the National Register of Historic Places by the United States Department of the Interior. As the Chelsea's owner Stanley Bard, a youthful 60-year-old, sits behind his cluttered desk, he speaks proudly of his ongoing friendship with his clientele, whom he describes as "the intelligentsia, the poet, writer, playwright, dancer, artist, painter, sculptor." Bard revels in the building's history.

The Chelsea Hotel was built in 1884 as an apartment building—it was the first building in New York to have 12 stories and penthouses. After going bankrupt in 1903, reopening as a hotel in 1905 and going bankrupt again in 1939, it was purchased by Bard's father, David. Stanley took over operation of the hotel in 1957, and has been joined by his son, David, and his daughter Michelle. In the lobby, dust has settled on the dried eucalyptus, long-since arranged in a

green jar on one of two silver-and glass deco coffee tables in the lobby. Blue leather benches are arranged around the fireplace, which is flanked by matching griffin statuettes. The walls, a single window, and the ceiling are crowded with an array of art, much of which has been donated by residents, or even bartered for rent—which, at $1,000 a month for a tiny loft, is expensive, even by New York standards.

But legend and rent don't make the hotel an exclusive haven for the elite. From among the 70% of its 250 rooms occupied by long-term residents, there are a number of fairly

Speak, preview issue

Magazine spreads
ART DIRECTOR/DESIGNER   Martin Venezky
CONTRIBUTING DESIGNERS   Bob Aufuldish, Fred Bower, Bill Bowers,
Elliott Peter Earls, Geoff Kaplan
PHOTOGRAPHERS   Melodie McDaniel, Michael Darter, Paige Stuart
PRINCIPAL TYPEFACES   Univers, Bodoni, Franklin Gothic, Spartan Classified,
Century Expanded, custom-made for the project
PUBLISHER   Dan Rolleri

USA, 1995

JIMMY SMITH / IF HE WAS BORN BEFORE YOUR FATHER;

temperature

Here's what matters. There are hot organ solos and then there are *burning* organ solos. Jimmy Smith plays the second kind. When Smith gets cooking on one of his infamous solos, it sounds as though he were hacking away at the keys of his organ with a fiery axe, simultaneously dousing the crackling Leslie speaker with gasoline and selling the beast alive. Fluid, lyrical improvisations skate across the keys with amazing grace, and then attack you sideways, with Smith's trademark percussive rabbit-punch style. It can all be very dizzying as a listening experience, but it's also elegant, robust, and never too hokily jolly.

Marking Smith's return to Verve after a 23-year absence, *Damn!* features a host of jazz's young lions, including trumpeter Roy Hargrove, bassist Christian McBride, and guitarist Mark Whitfield, none of whom were born when Smith scored his first great successes in the mid 1950s and early 1960s. "This is more exciting than the old sessions," Smith says. "You're working with young guys, 22 or 23 years old, and they've mastered their horns already. It scares me that they know all these things. These guys have 'electrified me with the directions they go."

Smith covers a range of modern black music, from James Brown's classic "Papa's Got a Brand New Bag" to Dizzy Gillespie's hard-bopping "Woody 'n' You." *Damn!* also features two of the greatest drummers of all time, the ubiquitous Bernard Purdie, and the late Arthur Taylor, who contributed the final performances of his lifetime to the recording.

Unlike Herbie Hancock, (whose "Watermelon Man" is covered here with jittery aplomb and one of the tightest, lowest and juiciest grooves of the last 10 years) Smith does not pander to the beats and music that came after him. While Hancock's most recent album, *Dis Is Da Drum*, got lost in a mish-mash of contemporary loops and drum programming, Smith delivers the goods in a raw, timeless fashion. You won't confuse his sound for that of any of Smith's many imitators, because he doesn't try to give it a '90s spin. He's smart. With so many bands sampling him and struggling to cop that famous and famous Jimmy Smith Style, why would he try to emulate them?

And if anyone ever tells you they don't like jazz because it's too stodgy or fancy or old fashioned, do them a favor: Lay some Jimmy Smith on them. And watch their head start to rock, and their eyes start to smile, and their mouths say...

BUT he's funkier than your little brother's gym socks, and here's how you know: take the funk taste test. Grab a copy of *Damn!* (Verve), the veteran jazz/funk/R&B organ-player's most recent album, and compare it to the latest by BRAND NEW HEAVIES, US3, or any other new jack acid jazz group you care to imagine. Notice how Smith sounds *lovely* like butter and the competition seems like pure Parkay by comparison?

Born in Norristown, Pennsylvania, on December 8, 1928, James Oscar "Jimmy" Smith was nine years old the day he won first place on Major Bowes Amateur Hour radio show, playing boogie-woogie piano. "I had piano books on the seat underneath me so I could reach the keys," recalled of that seminal moment. "Once I got going I didn't want to stop. The announcer was saying 'Ladies and gentlemen, this kid's on fire. He's burning the place up.'" Many years later, after a stint in the navy, Smith was playing with the R&B group on a show known for its unassailable underground credibility (tapes of his shows circulate on the street for as much as $25 each.) "I try to keep my ears clean," says Red, "and listen for sounds that are different from others and can help lead off."

by Dimitri Ehrlich

---

who who is who is who is go-

by Dimitri Ehrlich

mannered, red-haired, Harlem resident, who turns into the TASmanian devil on a pair of turntables? He deconstructs the beats, putting them back together in syncopated collages of sound and noise, with rhyth-

...mic instincts to rival those of a master percussionist. And he is arguably the subject of more recorded shout-outs than anyone else in the world, hence his nickname "the Prop Master." Red gets his props from hundreds of emcees who owe him their first play, or simply respect his skill, his sensibility, and his staying power in an industry where three albums makes you a veteran. Over the course of a decade, he's been the first radio DJ to play dozens of hip-hop records that went on to become national hits. He has also been among the bravest and most eclectic program-mers, mixing everything from Hall & Oates, Men At Work, and the Rolling Stones into a rap show known for its unassailable underground credibility (tapes of his shows circulate on the street for as much as $25 each.) "I try to keep my ears clean," says Red, "and listen for sounds that are different from others and can help lead off."

Red also helped lead the rise of dancehall reggae, mixing rap's Jamaican counterpart into his shows as early as 1988. Last year he released an album for Epic Records entitled *Kool DJ Red Alert's Dancehall Show*, showcasing new dancehall talent, including Vicious, who went on to release a successful solo album. "A lot of people credit me for playing dance-hall reggae. I took a risk on it because Afrika Bambaataa showed me that you can combine any kind of music with hip-hop and rap sounds. But I had learned about this music anyway, before reggae. I had learned soca, calypso and meringue from my grandparents who come from Antigua."

Red began his career under the tutelage of one of rap's founding fathers, a Bronx-based Jamaican-American named Kool Herc, who knew about the dance hall reggae sound systems in Kingston. It was there that Jamaican emcees, known as toasters, began to develop their rapid patois boasting in the 1970s, around the same time that rap, dancehall's American cousin, was developing in New York City clubs such as Pippons, Superstar Cafe, and the Diplomat Hotel. There, Red heard pioneering DJs like the late Grandmaster Flowers, the late Charisma, Pete "DJ" Jones, Together Brothers, and, in the Bronx, Kool Herc. As disco and funk collided, Red Alert found his calling in the emergent music then called "hip-hop/bebop." In 1979 he joined Afrika Bambaataa's legendary Zulu Nation, as part of a group called Soulsonic Force. "There was a club called the Twilight Zone up on Jerome Avenue in the Bronx," says Red. "I came in there and it was like a whole different scene, because Herc was DJing and mixing the records back and forth, instead of one after the other. And that's what inspired me." By 1983, Red began broadcasting his own hip-hop show, and has since released several demos on his broadcasts. He still occasionally listens to the hundreds of demo tapes and records that he receives every week and he still lives in his parents' home on 113th Street. "I still live in the same neighborhood, still tend to people the same way. I feel better that way because I feel you'll be more respected when people see you don't change. A lot of people expect you to be fancy, riding big cars, living in a big house. I don't think that really gives you respect. Just remain as you are."

And what does the hip-hop avatar see for the future of the genre? Rap radio's least talkative DJ isn't telling. "You got to go with the people that create it. You can't say it, but you can play it."

who is who

Raygun's impact with readers, advertisers and the design community made it inevitable that others would attempt to apply its lessons. *Speak* magazine, published in San Francisco, is a quarterly review of fashion, lifestyle and the arts. Martin Venezky, art director for the preview issue, had created a number of pages for *Raygun* and his design for *Speak* achieves a balance between readability in the main copy and expression in its display typography and other visual devices. David Carson was appointed art director from the second issue.

The Downlow no. 6 — Hip-hop magazine cover and spread

DESIGNERS | Dominic Lippa, Mark Diaper, Rachel Dinnis, Michael Davies
DESIGN COMPANY | Lippa Pearce Design
PRINCIPAL TYPEFACE | Template Gothic
CLIENT | The Downlow

Great Britain, 1995

The Downlow no. 9

Hip-hop magazine cover and spread
DESIGNERS | Michael Davies, Mark Diaper, Birgit Eggers
PRINCIPAL TYPEFACES | Triplex, Citizen, OCRB, News Gothic
CLIENT | *The Downlow*

Great Britain, 1995

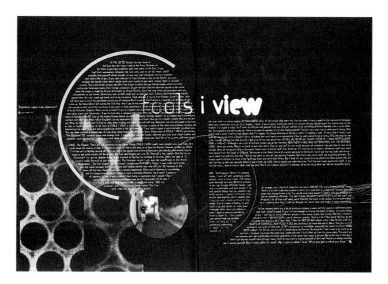

The Downlow no. 10

Hip-hop magazine spread
DESIGNERS | Michael Davies, Mark Diaper, Birgit Eggers,
MC Colosseum, Shaun O'Mara, Glen Thornley, Alan King
PRINCIPAL TYPEFACE | Template Gothic
CLIENT | *The Downlow*

Great Britain, 1996

Blah Blah Blah no. 1

Magazine cover and spread
ART DIRECTORS/DESIGNERS Chris Ashworth, Neil Fletcher, Amanda Sissons
DESIGN COMPANY Substance
PHOTOGRAPHER Alison Dyer
PRINCIPAL TYPEFACE DIN
CLIENT Ray Gun Publishing

Great Britain, 1996

Blah Blah Blah no. 2

Magazine spread
ART DIRECTORS/DESIGNERS | Chris Ashworth, Neil Fletcher, Amanda Sissons
DESIGN COMPANY | Substance
PHOTOGRAPHER | Joseph Cultice
PRINCIPAL TYPEFACE | Compacta
CLIENT | Ray Gun Publishing

Great Britain, 1996

Blah Blah Blah no. 3

Magazine spread
ART DIRECTORS/DESIGNERS | Chris Ashworth, Neil Fletcher, Amanda Sissons
DESIGN COMPANY | Substance
PHOTOGRAPHER | Kevin Westenberg
PRINCIPAL TYPEFACE | Univers
CLIENT | Ray Gun Publishing

Great Britain, 1996

Stella Artois Dry

	Print campaign
ART DIRECTOR	Simon Butler
DESIGNERS/ILLUSTRATORS	Whitney Lowe, Somi Kim, Lisa Nugent, James Moore
DESIGN COMPANY	ReVerb
PHOTOGRAPHER	Tim O. Sullivan (tattoo)
PRINCIPAL TYPEFACES	Abbess, Altoona, Acropilis, Dolmen Decorated, Egbert, Enlivan, Falstaff, Siena, Garage Gothic, Helvetica, Melody, Monster, Narly, Pinwheel, Phrastic,
AGENCY	Lowe Howard-Spink
CLIENT	Whitbread

Great Britain, 1995

The Bearded Lady

	Television commercial
DIRECTOR	Kinka Usher
ART DIRECTOR	Todd Grant
CREATIVE DIRECTOR	Bo Coyner
DESIGNER/ANIMATOR	Alexei Tylevich
AGENCY	Goodby, Silverstein & Partners
PRINCIPAL TYPEFACES	Custom-made for the project
CLIENT	Sega

USA, 1994

The bizarre narrative of Sega's
commercial for a 32-bit game system
was set in an amusement park freak show.
Alexei Tylevich's animated typographic
segments for both 30 and 60 second
versions reflect the hallucinatory theme
of the commercial's live action.

Print campaign

DESIGNER Simon Taylor
DESIGN COMPANY Tomato
AGENCY Bates Dorland
PHOTOGRAPHER Simon Taylor
PRINCIPAL TYPEFACES DIN Engschrift, Aachen
CLIENT Grolsch

Great Britain, 1995

it's easy to develop your 6th sense
with this simple exercise.

think of an image to stimulate all
five senses. this is the key to
awakening your 6th sense.

there is a suitable image pictured
here. as always, we've chosen it
completely at random.

fix this image in your mind's eye.
distinctive shape, isn't it?

imagine touching the condensation
dropping over the embossed
contours.

now listen. a pop and a slight clink.

esp for those who haven't got it yet.

1

2

3

think about its smell. a heady
aroma of hops and malt.

by now, your mouth may feel dry.
this is quite normal. just imagine
icy continental lager swooshing
over your taste buds.

...better?

well, since all 5 senses are now
fully stimulated, your 6th sense
should be stirring. the sense that
allows you to know the future.

for example, you know exactly
which lager you're going to ask for
later...

uncanny, isn't it?

4

5

6

Extra Sensory Perfection

Extra Sensory Perfection

some of the first recorded
examples of 6th sense
were the predictions of
nostradamus. the recent
discovery of his diary
provides a fascinating
insight into his working
methods:

wed: went to ye bar.
ordered a bottle of lager.
malt pleasing to ye eye.
ye guff waf embossed to
ye touch, and opened
with a most distinctive
pop clink.

ye smell brought to mind
hopf and malt, and ye
taste waf like ambrosia of
ye guff.

early ———— **esp**

suddenly, i felt a stirring
of my fisth fenfe, which i
attributed to ye
ftimulation of ye other
five. managed 300 yearf
of prediction before laft
ordert.

thurf: fomewhat hazy.
vaguely recall predicting
hitler. flared troufert and
ye end of ye world.

there was, of course, a
fatal flaw. he was drinking
grolsch instead of grolsch,
which wouldn't exist for
another 3 centuries. this is
why the world didn't blow
up in 1990, as predicted. a
point worth celebrating
with a stimulating flagon
or two, we feel.

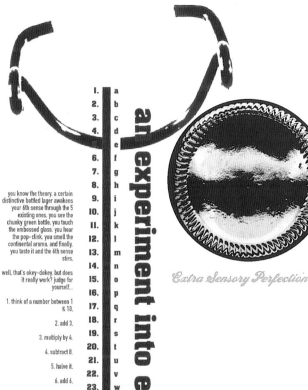

an experiment into esp

you know the theory. a certain distinctive bottled lager awakens your 6th sense through the 5 existing ones. you see the chunky green bottle. you touch the embossed glass. you hear the pop-clink. you smell the continental aroma. and finally, you taste it and the 6th sense stirs.

well, that's okey-dokey. but does it really work? judge for yourself...

1. think of a number between 1 & 10.

2. add 3.

3. multiply by 4.

4. subtract 8.

5. halve it.

6. add 6.

7. halve it again.

8. add 3.

9. subtract the number you first thought of.

10. match the remaining number to its corresponding letter on the mystic chart.

now concentrate on a premium lager beginning with that letter.

absolutely correct. your 6th sense is alive and well. it's probably thirsty, too. so why not pop open a chilled bottle of 7-18-15-12-19-3-8?

1.	a
2.	b
3.	c
4.	d
	e
6.	f
7.	g
8.	h
9.	i
10.	j
11.	k
12.	l
13.	m
14.	n
15.	o
16.	p
17.	q
18.	r
19.	s
20.	t
21.	u
22.	v
23.	w
24.	x
25.	y
26.	z

Extra Sensory Perfection

Foggie Bummer

Commercial for a spoken-word radio station

DESIGNER Jonathan Barnbrook

WRITERS Lindsey Redding, Adrian Jefferey

AGENCY Faulds

PRINCIPAL TYPEFACES Clarendon, Times, Franklin Gothic, Eurostile

CLIENT BBC Radio Scotland

Great Britain, 1995

True Romance

Commercial for a spoken-word radio station
DESIGNER / Jonathan Barnbrook
WRITERS / Lindsey Redding, Adrian Jeffereys
AGENCY / Faulds
PRINCIPAL TYPEFACES \ Manson, Bastard, Nixonscript
CLIENT \ BBC Radio Scotland

Great Britain, 1995

Vicks Action

Commercial for a cold remedy
DESIGNER Jonathan Barnbrook
WRITERS Stuart Newman, Julian Borra
AGENCY Leo Burnett
PRINCIPAL TYPEFACES Letter Gothic, VAG Rounded, Isonorm
CLIENT Procter & Gamble

Great Britain, 1995

context;

flux

i think of civilization as a grand experiment to see if anything systematic can be done to promote kindness and sanity in human affairs. the network infrastructure developments of the next decade should comprise a codification of what can be learned from this experiment thus far. jaron lanier

we all belong somewhere

The subject of MTV's first European music awards was "global communication" and the designers' aim was to portray this in typography and image. Working collaboratively, they visualised the collage of quotations and specially written texts as an emotive, flowing stream of consciousness, rather than as a series of separate and possibly disjointed spreads. To enhance the intended humanistic feel, most of the artwork was originated by hand and a variety of papers was used.

Global Communication: Channel Your Experience

Spreads from a brochure for the MTV Music Awards

DESIGN DIRECTORS / John Warwicker, Simon Taylor

DESIGNERS / John Warwicker, Simon Taylor, Chris Ashworth, David Smith

WRITER / Michael Horsham

DESIGN COMPANIES / Tomato, Invisible

PRINCIPAL TYPEFACES / Cooper Black, Compacta, Clarendon, Courier, DIN

CLIENT / MTV Europe

Great Britain, 1994

The complexity I'm interested
I'm not so much interested
layers of meaning . . . I think
society because the conten
complex. Simple black and wh
Graphic design that tries to m
anybody any real benefit. Soc
to deal with the subtlety, con
contemporary life . . . it is po
both complexity and intelli

I'M REALLY I
THIS CONCEF
SURFACES".
MYSTICAL EL
INDUSTRIA
OR ALLOYS, CL

Jonathan Barnbrook

necessarily going to get it the first time you look at it.
meaning, though the communication process isn't so direct that you are
There's a reason for the way I do things and if you look I hope you'll get the
to say something yourself, you might as well say something you believe in . . .
Most of the time the message isn't worth saying. So when you do get a chance

l in is complexity of meaning.
in the layers of form as the
k this approach fits modern
mporary world is subtle and
nite dualisms no longer work.
ake things simple is not doing
iety needs to understand how
mplexity and contradiction in
ssible and necessary to have
igibility in graphic design. *Katherine McCoy*

'NTERESTED IN
'T OF "LIVING
. . IN MERGING
EMENTS WITH
L ELEMENTS
ULTURAL ALLOYS.

P. SCOTT MAKELA

CULTURE:

institutional

I am worth *loving*

I BELIEVE *in who I am. I practice safe sex so I can stay healthy. I wouldn't want to face the physical and emotional ordeal that comes with having AIDS.*

What are you worth?

The designers conceived a campaign to reach populations under-served or ignored by San Francisco's AIDS prevention literature. Each poster combines an honest portrait of a local individual, based on the designers' interviews, with the person's own answer to the question. The typography purposely avoids the customary slickness of most citywide advertising in an attempt to capture a hands-on, spontaneous visual language that will appeal to the target group.

What Are You Worth?

AIDS prevention poster
DESIGNERS / Martin Venezky, Raul Cabra
DESIGN COMPANY / Diseño
PHOTOGRAPHER / Leslie Hirsch
CLIENT / San Francisco AIDS Foundation

/ USA, 1995

Poster for World AIDS Day
DESIGNER Joseph Thomas
DESIGN COMPANY Push
ILLUSTRATORS Joseph Thomas, Patrice Gueroult
PRINCIPAL TYPEFACES Univers, Bureau Grotesque
CLIENT Akina Mama Wa Africa

Great Britain, 1994

Say vol. 3 no. 1

Magazine cover and spread aimed at a student/youth readership

DESIGNERS | Hal Wolverton, Pam Racs
DESIGN COMPANY | Johnson & Wolverton
PHOTOGRAPHER | Stephen Dupont
ILLUSTRATOR | Pam Racs
CLIENT | Amnesty International

USA, 1994

Rwanda:

A Country Riven by Hatred and Fear

BY DIANA QUICK
PHOTOGRAPHY BY STEPHEN DUPONT

Say vol. 3 no. 4

Magazine cover and spread aimed at a student/youth readership

DESIGNERS Hal Wolverton, Kat Saito, Robin Muir
DESIGN COMPANY Johnson & Wolverton
CLIENT Amnesty International

USA, 1995

It's About Change

AIDS fundraising poster
DESIGNERS | Richard Bates, Rob Eberhart
DESIGN COMPANY | Bates Hori
PHOTOGRAPHERS | Richard Bates, Allen Hori
PRINCIPAL TYPEFACES | Goudy, Helvetica
CLIENT | Lifebeat

USA, 1994

46th Spring National Viewing Sessions

Catalogue cover
DESIGNER \ Joseph Thomas
DESIGN COMPANY \ Push
PRINCIPAL TYPEFACE \ Triplex
CLIENT \ British Film Institute

Great Britain, 1995

Ruth **MYLIUS**

PHOTOPSY
PHOTOPSY

 f.stop Gallery & Darkrooms, Green Park Station, Bath, ba1 1jb.

MYLIUS
MYLIUS

Exhibition dates:
sat 8 October - sat 19 November
1994

Opening times:
tuesday 6pm - 9pm
wednesday, friday & saturday 10am
-6pm
thursday 10am - 9pm

Exhibition preview:
saturday 8 October 6 - 8pm

f.Stop Gallery & Darkrooms, Green Park Station, Bath, ba1 1jb.

INVESTMENT
SOUTH WEST ARTS

Green Park
STATION
BATH LIMITED

Design: Julian Harriman-Dickinson

Photopsy

Poster for photographic exhibition
DESIGNER Julian Harriman-Dickinson
PHOTOGRAPHER Ruth Mylius
PRINCIPAL TYPEFACES Custom-made for the project, Monaco

Concert poster
DESIGNER Cornel Windlin
ILLUSTRATOR Andreas Gefe
PRINCIPAL TYPEFACES Custom-made for the project
CLIENT Rote Fabrik

Switzerland, 1994

Abstract

...part of the Baltimore Playwrights Festival. ABSTRACT PURPLE. An   original play by   Steve Harper.

(Fells Point Corner Theatre)

JULY 15   3¹   CALL   2 76.   ●   78 ³ 7   Directed by Miriam Bazensky.

Purple

Abstract Purple

Theatre poster
DESIGNER Paul Sahre
PRINCIPAL TYPEFACES Garamond, Futura
CLIENT Fells Point Corner Theatre

USA, 1994

Hamlet

Theatre programme

DESIGNERS / Andrew Johnson, Nick Oates

PRINCIPAL TYPEFACES / Gil Sans, Ehrhardt

CLIENT / Young Vic Theatre Company

Great Britain, 1994

The pages of the wire-bound programme are cut to form a book within a book, allowing viewers to rearrange the pages in any number of permutations and engaging them in a physical, visual, textual and typographic exploration of the complexities of Shakespeare's tragedy.

To keep colour printing costs down, Zeebelt Theater posters are conceived by Studio Dumbar as extended series. A photograph is printed in quantity and the monthly calendar or information for a specific event – such as The Hague's "Day of Architecture" – is silkscreened on top. Studio interns undertake many experimental typographic interpretations of the same base image.

Theatre posters
DESIGNER | Martin Venezky
DESIGN COMPANY | Studio Dumbar
PHOTOGRAPHER | Lex van Pieterson
PRINCIPAL TYPEFACE | Frutiger
CLIENT | Zeebelt Theater

The Netherlands, 1993

Radix Matrix: The Architecture of Daniel Libeskind

Exhibition poster
DESIGNER Cornel Windlin
PRINCIPAL TYPEFACES Custom-made for the project
CLIENT Museum für Gestaltung, Zurich

Switzerland, 1994

Walker Art Center
and the Minnesota Composers Forum
present

Direct from New York's acclaimed Bang on a Can Festival, an annual celebration of explosive avant-garde composition, comes

this three-hour concert by the festival's star performers.

The lineup includes some of the country's most accomplished musical blowers, pounders, pluckers, pullers, sliders, scrapers, and grunters—not to mention strikers of such objects as car parts, pots, and bones.

BANG
(BANG)
(!) on
CAN ALL-STARS

mini music marathon

" an irreverent boundary smashing event ... an array of avant-garde musical styles and a lively burst of contemporary fireworks. "
— *New York Times*

Maya Beiser

Robert Black

David Lang

Lisa Moore

Steve Schick

Mark Stewart and

Evan Ziporyn ...

... will offer pieces by nationally known composers, including premieres of works by Louis Andriessen, Michael Gordon, and Eleanor Hovda, as well as compositions by David Lang and Frederic Rzewski.

8 pm

$ 10 ($8)
Saturday, November 21, 1992
Walker Auditorium
For tickets, call the Walker box office at
375-7622.

($) = price for Walker and MCF members, seniors, AFDC cardholders, groups of 10 or more

Bang on the Can

Poster for a "noise" music event

DESIGNER   Susan LaPorte
DESIGN COMPANY   Walker Art Center Design Department
ILLUSTRATOR   Susan LaPorte
PRINCIPAL TYPEFACE Big Girl Bold

A Lie of the Mind

Theatre poster
DESIGNERS | Paul Sahre, David Plunkert
PRINCIPAL TYPEFACE | Futura
CLIENT | Fells Point Corner Theatre

USA, 1993

BY SAM SHEPHARD

A LIE

DIRECTED BY DENISE RATAJCZAK

OF THE

MIND

BALTIMORE PREMIERE

276-7837

FELLS POINT

JANUARY 15 THRU FEBRUARY 21

CORNER THEATRE

Spaced Out

Cover and spread from a leaflet for a series of talks on architecture
DESIGNER Jonathan Barnbrook
PRINCIPAL TYPEFACES Delux, Perpetua
CLIENT Institute of Contemporary Arts

Great Britain, 1995

Spaced Out 2

Cover and spread from a leaflet for a series of talks on architecture
DESIGNER Jonathan Barnbrook
PRINCIPAL TYPEFACES Bell Gothic, Clarendon, Bodoni, Cooper Black
CLIENT Institute of Contemporary Arts

Great Britain, 1995

2 NOVEMBER
1994

18 FEBRUARY
1995

The Scapegoat

Cover and spread from a leaflet for a series of talks on social scapegoats

DESIGNER / Jonathan Barnbrook

PHOTOGRAPHER / Tomoko Yoneda

PRINCIPAL TYPEFACES / Scala, False Idol

CLIENT / Institute of Contemporary Arts

Great Britain, 1994

"AND THE **goat** shall bear upon him all their iniquities unto a land not inhabited."

from show trials to fictional heroes. a series on the social implications of scapegoating, looking forward to a major conference in 1995.

2 NOVEMBER 19.30HRS
SHOW TRIALS
The show trial is a prime instrument of state in its search for scapegoats. The media furore and public outrage surrounding judicial cases such as the Guildford Four, Winston Silcott and, in Israel, John Demjanjuk makes the possibility of fair trial seem unlikely if not impossible. Yoram Sheftel, who successfully defended John Demjanjuk, the Ukrainian-American auto worker accused of being 'Ivan the Terrible', talks with Ronan Bennett, author of *Double Jeopardy: The retrial of the Guildford Four* (Penguin), and George Silcott, brother of Winston Silcott whose conviction for the murder of PC Keith Blakelock was quashed by the Court of Appeal. Chaired by Geoffrey Robertson QC, author of the seminal work on civil liberties *Freedom, The Individual and the Law*.

24 NOVEMBER 19.30HRS
BETWEEN BLIGH AND BOSNIA:
VIOLENCE, FICTION AND THE SCAPEGOAT
Why was the decent officer Captain Bligh of *The Bounty* cast as the arch-villain? Slavoj Zizek, of the Institute of Social Sciences in Ljubljana, shows how the need for scapegoats arises when the symbolic fiction regulating society is under threat. The experience of post-Yugoslav war and the rise of 'irrational' violence in late capitalism provides the context for his new book *The Metastases of Enjoyment* (Verso).

30 NOVEMBER 19.30HRS
AIDS AND INIQUITY
On the eve of World AIDS Day, a distinguished panel discuss AIDS scapegoating. With: Simon Watney on the politics of epidemeology; Simon Taylor of the Haemophiliac Society; Rosalind Harrison, co-author of *Aids, Africa and Racism*; Jonathan Grimshaw of Body Positive and Caroline Guinness of Positively Women. Chaired by Simon Garfield, author of *The End of Innocence, Britain in the Time of AIDS* (Faber).

TICKETS £5.50 [£4.50 MEMBERS AND CONCESSIONS]

BOX OFFICE 071 930 3647

6 DECEMBER 19.30HRS
TALKING THE DOG
"Our best hope, perhaps our only hope, is to identify, and name, the opposite of a dog" IAIN SINCLAIR

In one generation, dogs, and pit bulls in particular, have gone from being 'man's best friend' to his most convenient scapegoat. From Steven Berkoff's *One Dog Show* to Iain Sinclair's dissection of dog culture, the canine world is the repository for all that is irrationally vicious. Asking why it is dogs rather than their owners that are now on trial, and how this comments on current anxieties around masculinity and class are novelist Iain Sinclair, Stewart Home, Neoist and author of *Defiant Pose* and Ben Watson, author of *Frank Zappa, The Negative Dialectics of Poodle Play*.

6 DECEMBER 18–22.00HRS THEATRE
ADMISSION FREE WITH TALKING THE DOG TICKET
OR WITH ICA DAY MEMBERSHIP £1.50
DOING THE DOG: CRANKY DISCO,
INDEX THEATRE, BLAST THEORY
Offering an inspired commentary on our Dog Debate, live art practitioners offer new dog-themed work: Cranky Disco wrestles with her staffordshire bull terrier in its cage; Index Theatre present material from their large-scale video installation, *The Alphabet of Dogs*; Blast Theory show images from *Stampede*: as a performer makes molotov cocktails watched by a boxer on a concrete chair.

9 th Annual

Port Clinton **ART FESTIVAL**

SECOND

CENTRAL

FIRST

LAUREL

August 28 and 29, 1993
10 a.m. to 6 p.m.
Downtown Highland Park
Illinois
All Media Juried Show featuring more than 230 Artists
Free Admission
Information: 708.433.799.

Port Clinton Art Festival

Poster
DESIGNER Stephen Farrell
DESIGN COMPANY Stephen Farrell Design
PRINCIPAL TYPEFACES Carmella, Keedy Sans, Triplex
CLIENT Highland Park Arts League

USA, 1993

Living Surfaces

Conference poster
DESIGNER P. Scott Makela
DESIGN COMPANY Words and Pictures for Business and Culture
PHOTOGRAPHERS Rik Sferra, P. Scott Makela
PRINCIPAL TYPEFACES Officina, VAG Rounded, Barmeno
CLIENT American Center for Design

USA, 1993

body

the 25th anniversary calarts

soul

december 8 + 9 + 10 1994
modular theatre at 8pm *tickets $10 general $3 alumni $2 students at door*

ensemble

PRESENTS

a celebration dedicated to those dance alumni who we have lost to *aids*

featuring alumni

pain

ecstasy

Dance Ensemble

Poster to announce a concert dedicated to dance alumni who died from AIDS

DESIGNER Jennifer Moody
DESIGN COMPANY Office of Public Affairs, California Institute of the Arts
PHOTOGRAPHER Steven Gunther
PRINCIPAL TYPEFACES Dorchester Script, Scala, Skelter, What the Hell
CLIENT School of Dance, California Institute of the Arts

USA, 1994

frédérique desfossez   présente

SOLO

3.–8. MAI '94 20.30 h   TACHELES theatersaal
oranienburgerstr. 54–56, 10117 berlin, kartenvorverkauf: 2826185

sasha waltz berlin

adria ferrali florenz

kitt johnson kopenhagen

+ newcoming artists…

Projekt: Solo

Concert poster
DESIGNER Anusch Thielbeer
DESIGN COMPANY Grappa Design
PHOTOGRAPHER Georgij Zimin (1923)
PRINCIPAL TYPEFACES Trade Gothic, Anu Font
CLIENT Kunsthaus Tacheles

Film festival poster
DESIGNERS / Heike Grebin, Andreas Trogisch
DESIGN COMPANY / Grappa Design
PHOTOGRAPHER/ILLUSTRATOR / Andreas Trogisch
PRINCIPAL TYPEFACE / Eurostile
CLIENT \ Internationale Kurzfilmtage Oberhausen

Germany, 1995

Bauhaus Kammerkonzert

Concert posters

DESIGNERS Daniela Haufe, Detlef Fiedler

DESIGN COMPANY Cyan

PRINCIPAL TYPEFACE Akzidenz Grotesk

CLIENT Bauhaus, Dessau

Germany, 1994

OPER NACH DEM FILM VON
JEAN COCTEAU

Europäische Erstaufführung

PHILIP GLASS
ORPHÉE

Freiluftvorstellungen im Renaissance-Schloßhof Weikersheim/Württemberg:
31.7.–2.8., 4.8., 6.8.–7.8., 8.8.1993

Begin: 21.00 Uhr

Musik: Philip Glass
Libretto: Nach dem Drehbuch von Jean Cocteau
bearbeitet von Robert Brustein
herausgegeben von Philip Glass
Copyright 1993 Dunvagen Music Publishers, Inc.

Schirmherrin: Bundesministerin Dr. Angela Merkel

Musikalische Leitung: Dennis Russell Davies

Regie: Birgitta Trommler

Bühnenbild: Thomas Pekny

Kostüme: Barbara Luschenkohl

Streicherchester der Musikakademie Litauen

Solisten und Instrumentalisten der 38. Internationalen Sommerkurse Schloß Weikersheim

Eine Produktion der Jeunesses Musicales Deutschland, Marktplatz 12,
D–97990 Weikersheim, Telefon: 07934/280, Telefax: 07934/8526

JEUNESSES
MUSICALES
DEUTSCHLAND

	Orphée
	Opera poster
DESIGNERS	David Ellis, Andy Altmann
DESIGN COMPANY	Why Not Associates
PHOTOGRAPHER	Image Library
PRINCIPAL TYPEFACE	Doddy
CLIENT	Lippert Wilkens Partner
	Great Britain, 1993

Turangalîla

Concert poster
DESIGNER | Andrew Johnson
PRINCIPAL TYPEFACE | Univers
CLIENT | Royal Philharmonic Orchestra

Great Britain, 1993

culture

Slide installation for Kobe Fashion Museum

DESIGNERS Andy Altmann, David Ellis, Patrick Morrissey
DESIGN COMPANY Why Not Associates
PHOTOGRAPHERS Rocco Redondo, Richard Woolf, PhotoDisc
PRINCIPAL TYPEFACE Monotype Grotesque
CLIENT Dai Nippon

Great Britain, 1995

Since form cannot be separated from content and since form itself carries meaning, then the idea is, in fact, structured and informed by its presentation.

Just as the invisible typeface is an impossibility, neither can form be invisible.

Louise Sandhaus

THEN

NOW

I love the "POST-MODERN PLURALISM": idea of a post-historical forever: mix and match, past and present, high and low, regular and irregular, "inept" and professional, raw and cooked and everything in between, inside and outsider ... and so on and on and on and on.

Edward Fella

form

We use styles like maniacs but we never use them lock, stock and barrel. We would usually manipulate them to create some kind of tension. No style is either good or bad; it's just another style — whether you use it wholesale or not.

Lorraine Wild

WHY IS "CUTTING EDGE" USUALLY

SYNONYMOUS WITH ILLEGIBILITY?

WHAT WOULD HAPPEN IF THE TWO TERMS

"hip" and **"hard to read"**

WERE UNCOUPLED?

Can a text be both readerly and experimental?

J. Abbott Miller

CULTURE:

educational/publishing

THE HIGHWAY, WHERE THERE IS A SIGN WITH THE PYRAMIDS AND THE WORDS "VISIT EGYPT," AND A LITTLE ICE-CREAM WAGON TRIES TO PASS A BIG TRUCK LADEN WITH INSTALLMENTS OF HIS STILL, A PERIODICAL ENCYCLOPEDIA that comes out in paperback, but then it puts its brakes on because its visibility is blocked by a cloud of bees WHICH CROSSES THE ROAD COMING FROM A ROW OF HIVES IN A FIELD FROM WHICH SURELY A QUEEN BEE IS FLYING AWAY, drawing behind her a swarm in the direction opposite to the smoke of the train, which has reappeared at the other end of the tunnel, so you can see hardly anything thanks to the cloudy stream of bees and coal smoke, EXCEPT A FEW YARDS FARTHER UP THERE IS A PEASANT BREAKING THE GROUND WITH HIS MATTOCK and, UNAWARE, HE BRINGS TO LIGHT AND REBURIES A FRAGMENT OF A NEOLITHIC MATTOCK SIMILAR TO HIS OWN, IN A GARDEN THAT SURROUNDS AN ASTRONOMICAL observatory with its telescopes aimed at the sky and on whose threshold the keeper's daughter sits reading the horoscopes in a weekly whose cover displays the face of the star of Cleopatra: I see all this and I feel no amazement because making the shell implied also making the honey in the wax comb and the coal and the telescopes and the reign of Cleopatra AND THE FILMS ABOUT CLEOPATRA AND THE PYRAMIDS AND THE DESIGN OF THE ZODIAC OF THE CHALDEAN ASTROLOGERS AND THE WARS AND EMPIRES HERODOTUS SPEAKS OF AND THE WORDS WRITTEN BY HERODOTUS AND THE WORKS WRITTEN IN ALL LANGUAGES INCLUDING THOSE OF SPINOZA IN DUTCH and the fourteen-line summary of Spinoza's life and works in the installment of the encyclopedia in the truck passed by the ice-cream wagon, and so I feel as if, in making the shell, I had also made the rest. I look around, and whom am I looking for? SHE IS STILL THE ONE I SEEK; I'VE BEEN IN LOVE FOR five hundred million years, AND IF I SEE A DUTCH GIRL ON THE SAND WITH A BEACHBOY WEARING A GOLD CHAIN AROUND HIS NECK AND SHOWING HER THE SWARM OF BEES TO FRIGHTEN HER, THERE SHE IS I RECOGNIZE HER FROM HER INIMITABLE WAY OF RAISING ONE SHOULDER UTIL IT ALMOST TOUCHES HER CHEEK, I'M ALMOST SURE, OR RATHER I'D SAY ABSOLUTELY SURE IF IT WEREN'T FOR A CERTAIN resemblance THAT I FIND ALSO IN THE DAUGHTER OF THE KEEPER OF THE OBSERVATORY, AND THE PHOTOGRAPH OF THE ACTRESS MADE UP AS CLEOPATRA, OR PERHAPS IN CLEOPATRA AS SHE REALLY WAS IN PERSON, FOR WHAT PART OF THE TRUE CLEOPATRA THEY NAY EVERY representation of Cleopatra contains, or in the queen bee flying at the head of the swarm with that forward impetuousness, or in the paper woman cut out and pasted on the plastic windshield of the little ice-cream wagon, wearing a bathing suit like the Dutch girl on the beach near a little transistor radio in the voice of a woman singing. THE SAME VOICE THAT THE ENCYCLOPEDIA TRUCK DRIVER HEARS OVER HIS RADIO, AND THE SAME ONE IM NOW SURE I'VE HEARD FOR FIVE MILLION YEARS, IT IS SURELY SHE I HEAR SINGING AND whose image I look for all around, seeing only gulls uniplanning on the surface of the sea where a school of anchovies glistens and for a moment I am certain I recognize HER IN A FEMALE GULL, AND A MOMENT LATER I SUSPECT THAT INSTEAD SHE'S AN ANCHOVY, THOUGH SHE MIGHT JUST AS WELL BE ANY QUEEN OR SLAVE-GIRL NAMED BY HERODOTUS OR only hinted at in the pages of the volume LEFT TO MARK THE SEAT OF THE READER WHO HAS STEPPED INTO THE CORRIDOR OF THE TRAIN TO STRIKE UP A CONVERSATION WITH THE PARTY OF DUTCH TOURISTS; I might say I am in love with each of those girls and at the same time I am sure of being in love always with her alone. And the more I torment myself with love for each of them, the less I can bring myself to say to them, whom I recognize so well, *"Here I am,"* afraid of being mistaken and even more afraid that she is mistaken, taking me for somebody else, for somebody who, for all she knows of me, might easily take my place, for example THE BEACHBOY WITH THE GOLD CHAIN, OR THE DIRECTOR OF THE OBSERVATORY, OR A GULL, OR A MALE ANCHOVY, on the reader of Herodotus, or Herodotus himself, OR THE VENDOR OF ICE CREAM, WHO HAS COME DOWN TO THE BEACH ALONG A DUSTY ROAD AMONG THE PRICKLY PEARS AND IS NOW SURROUNDED BY THE DUTCH GIRLS IN THEIR BATHING SUITS, OR SPINOZA, OR THE TRUCK DRIVER WHO IS TRANSPORTING THE LIFE AND WORKS OF SPINOZA SUMMARIZED AND REPEATED TWO THOUSAND TIMES, OR ONE OF THE drones dying at the bottom of the hive after having fulfilled his role in the continuation of the species.)

When we shower the design periodicals and quality newspapers with angry complaints about the blowsy bugler of BT, we are still missing the point. True, the BT style is an even more footling bit of nonsense than the Prudential popinjay, also from the same design office. But any corporate identity that puts itself about as ostentatiously as these two is offensive, whatever it looks like.

In a lecture delivered at Brunswick in May 1910, he stated: "It is particularly important for Germany, which has now achieved political power, also to win power in artistic areas...In this way, German art and technology will work towards one goal: towards the power of the German nation, which reveals itself in a rich material life ennobled by intellectually refined design." So here's our paragon: FRIGHTENINGLY WELL DESIGNED. So here's our paragon: corporate identity is infused with over-weaning, elitist notions of power and the imposition of order by the visionary few.

"is infused with over-weaning, elitist notions of power and the imposition of power by the visionary few."

Yet in order to represent everything, corporate identities become too diffuse, too bland, too all-encompassing.

"visual babel"

make every effort to see that his creation reaches out to the viewer with meaning."

Emigre no. 21

Magazine spreads showing projects by
California Institute of the Arts students
GUEST EDITOR   Jeffery Keedy
DESIGNERS   Margo Johnson, Gail Swanlund
CLIENT   Emigre Graphics

EDITOR | Rudy VanderLans
WRITER/DESIGNER | Anne Burdick
PRINCIPAL TYPEFACES | Clarendon, Sabbath Black
CLIENT | Emigre Graphics

USA, 1992

Already a significant force as the 1990s began, Rudy VanderLans's *Emigre* has achieved a thoughtfulness, consistency and rigour in its exploration of experimental typography that is without equal in magazine publishing. Completely redesigned from issue to issue, sometimes by guest editors, the magazine uses the type designs of its partner company, Emigre Fonts, to demonstrate that new approaches to page structure and textual flow can be applied in a way that both encourages and enhances the experience of reading.

Emigre no. 27, "+ David Carson"

Magazine page showing an
abstract type construction
EDITOR/DESIGNER | Rudy VanderLans
PRINCIPAL TYPEFACES | From *Raygun*
CLIENT | Emigre Graphics

USA, 1993

Emigre no. 32

Magazine pages

EDITOR/DESIGNER | Rudy VanderLans
DESIGNER AT LARGE | Gail Swanlund
ILLUSTRATOR | Brian Schorn
PRINCIPAL TYPEFACES | Matrix, Template Gothic
CLIENT | Emigre Graphics

USA, 1994

Emigre no. 28, "Broadcast"

Magazine page

GUEST EDITOR/DESIGNER | Gail Swanlund
PRINCIPAL TYPEFACES | OutWest, Citizen
CLIENT | Emigre Graphics

USA, 1993

RADICAL COMMODITIES

By Rudy VanderLans

The other day, I was reading an article about the Bauhaus by Dietmar Winkler. In it Winkler suggests that the Bauhaus legend is largely based upon myth that has obscured many truths about the Bauhaus. For instance, none of the Bauhaus ideologies, he says, originated at other schools or movements, such as the Constructivists, Futurists and De Stijl. He also points out the enormous gap that existed between the Bauhaus ideologies and the public, resulting in the design of products equally remote from the public's needs and users. Summing it all up, Winkler writes that **"When Hannes Meyer replaced Gropius as a director of the school, his critical assessment was that its reputation outstripped manifold the quality of the work produced. He attributed this to the unparalleled public relations effort."**

I don't know whether this is a correct assessment or not, but what struck me about this article was how much Winkler's observations regarding the Bauhaus myth could, to an extent, be said of Emigre as well. First of all, on more than one occasion, Emigre has received credit (or blame) for what were essentially the ideas of others whose work we published in our magazine. Secondly, like the Bauhaus, we are also ferocious promoters

*Dietmar Winkler,
Morality and Myth:
The Bauhaus Reassessed.
Looking Closer:
Critical Writings on
Graphic Design,
New York, Allworth Press,
1994, p.49*

Putch Tu

In the early 1980s, I moved to San Francisco, a place I'd been dreaming of since I was eight. This was after working for a short time in beautiful, postnuclear downtown Detroit, and after a stint in Dallas, which was, at the time, the murder capital of the US. When my friend Wild Bill (thusly named because he isn't) and I landed, it was very late at night, so we stopped at the only place open at three in the morning, a Vietnamese noodle bar on Broadway. It was a time when the Haight was becoming yuppified, when the Silicon Valley was burgeoning, when I picked up one of the first issues of Emigre. Back then, Emigre had an interesting mix of literature (an excerpt of JG Ballard's Crash, I think), poetry, art, and was not yet a tool of the design cognoscenti. There were five Michaels who seemed to rule the elitist and provincial design world, and the saying went, if you shook any tree, four designers would fall out.

**From Technology to Community
Where do we go from here?
Young designers
and the contemporary state of
graphic design.
By
Matt Owens**

Digital technologies are a future within graphic design and have redefined the very shape of the profession. The whole history and development of typographic conventions can now be broken with the click of a mouse, and this digital revolution has resulted in a visual renaissance unequaled in graphic design history. Simultaneously, the accessibility of the personal computer has thrown design into mediocrity—with the right software and a scanner, anyone can become a graphic designer. These technological developments have

[04]

RADICAL COMMODITIES

of our work. Whether it overshadows the quality of the work we produce is arguable, but what I do know is that without a focused public relations effort, Emigre would simply not exist. And perhaps the Bauhaus might not have existed either. Promoting our work, making our work public, in any way we can, is simply an inevitable necessity when publishing a magazine and selling typefaces for a living.

I've always been intrigued by the commercial aspects of publishing. I remember ten years ago when we started Emigre magazine, the one publication I was looking at a lot was RAW magazine. Although I was drawn to the work of Gary Panter, Charles Burns, Sue Coe, Joost Swarte and a host of others, and was moved by the subversive content of the work, I was even more curious to find out how RAW was made possible. I once visited Art Spiegelman and Francoise Mouly, the publishers, in their studio in New York, and I remember looking at all this social

That's when I began my multiple lives: a well-groomed, hopefully fashionable, wealth and status seeking designer during the day, hangin' at the Zeitgeist for relief at night, going to the Santa Cruz mountains to play with the intelligentsia from Berkeley and UCSC during the weekends. Most of the latter were fascist, vegetarian practicing, pagans who were a little too in touch with their inner children for my comfort, but then, the lunatic fringe came as a welcomed relief from the daily burden of makin' pretty pictures for the Man.

Spirit of the Times: Hangin' at the Zeitgeist

The Zeitgeist was a punk C&W (country and western) biker bar tucked under an on ramp of a freeway, somewhere near lower Hayes Valley and Market. It was as real a postmodern hybrid as it was dangerous; black

What do we go from here?

both widened and jeopardized the field as we know it. In the question arises, to what extent? At present, the continual search for new visual languages through technology has degenerated into easily appropriated formal conceits. In both the academy and the workplace, the question, "how did you do that?" has replaced notions of concept and content. For young designers weaned on Photoshop filters and Illustrator outlines, pushing the boundaries of text and image is an expected pursuit. These experiments in graphic form, divorced from

conceptual value and substantive content, can only text bar so long on the laurels of technology. In this world of staggering visual possibility, where do young designers look to bridge the gap between the conceptual and the digital? In his article Rick Smart, slow days, Design is Homework, Rick Poyner remarks that David Carson's embrace of corporate advertising serves "merely to conspire in and speed up the commodification of his own design process." This commodification is a direct consequence of the way we have

*Rick Poyner,
Rick Smart, Slow Days,
Design is Homework,
Eye30, no. 18,
Sep-Oct 1994, p.5*

[05]

---

count for the fact that so many of its readers feel quite uninhibited to write in and respond to everything from the writing to the use of the typefaces.

Ray Gun once and for all showed that the use of non-traditional typefaces and extreme typographic variations are possible within mainstream magazine publishing. Under the very gutsy art direction of David Carson, who invited various Caldets and Cranbrook graduates (including Teffal) to contribute to Ray Gun, anti-design had finally gone Big Time. And although there are many people who like to hate Ray Gun and quickly dismiss it as just another stylistic fad, I think it has greatly helped to expand the notion of legibility and magazine layout. All it took for some of the experiments to become accepted was the appropriate time, the right audience and an entrepreneur like Jarrett who could pull it all together.

Ch, Ch, Ch, Changes

Punk and Hip-hop were initially not accepted as credible musical forms, as distribution systems were created from the ground up. By doing so, these innovative musical styles forever changed the music industry in every aspect. They challenged not only how music sounded but also how it was created, produced and performed, and they also significantly changed how music was distributed and sold, creating many alternative economic environments.

This closely resembles the exciting changes that have taken place within typeface design and manufacture in the past five to ten years. The Macintosh computer has completely democratized the design and manufacture of fonts. Before, this had been the private domain of only a handful of large type foundries who owned the proprietary systems needed to turn a typeface design into a working product. In addition, with the recent possibility of selling typefaces electronically by modem, the Macintosh can now also provide the means of distribution, one of the most difficult hurdles to clear when you self-publish.

The acceptance of magazines like Ray Gun by both the design establishment and mainstream audiences, coupled in the ease with which one can technically produce fonts, has sparked a tremendous activity in typeface production, and graphic designers and magazines alike have recognized that designing and selling fonts can be a viable means of income.

The resulting availability of thousands of typefaces, with dozens added each month, is proof of a completely democratized field and shows us that graphic designers have used for more than the tried and the true. Although it would be easy to find a good deal wrong with the results, I would like to focus on the positives. No longer are graphic designers dependent upon the work of an elite of traditional typeface designers who produce fonts primarily for use in text. Today, graphic designers have access to nearly

---

always plagued the discourses of design. First is the easy slide from defining modernism in broad terms to embodiment in design as a style. **The notion of style is one of our more illusory concepts, and tends to be one of our more obvious stumbling blocks.** Combined with our tendency to discuss design in formalistic terms, we too easily separate form from content and from larger social, political, and economic issues, in turn isolating ourselves from the rich discourses surrounding other disciplines.

What seems to be problematic among designers is the relationship of theory to the practice and creation of artifacts. We seem to confuse theoretical considerations as a way to understand design with an application of them as methodologies for creation - the old theory/practice bifurcation. Someone did not sit in philosophical isolation to devise the idea of modernism that would be later applied to diverse disciplines. Rather, it was a

Where do we go from here?

provided new tone with the conceptual power of visual language.

End

*Matt Owens: Matt Owens@aol.com
Cranbrook Academy of Art, Design Department. criboogy@cranedine.com*

[6]

process and phenomenon that was already occurring in Western societies, the result of society's attempt to come to terms with secularism, industrialization, the move from agrarian to urban organizations, and a reconfiguration of power and economic relations that began to emerge in the nineteenth century. It signalled an epochal shift in consciousness in response to momentous social, political, and economic orders. Philosophers and theoreticians named and characterized what already existed, took that, and pointed toward new directions of thinking and action, as did workers, artists, and the ruling class. We look to theoreticians because they can clarify very complex phenomena and perhaps point toward recommended directions of action, not because they necessarily have a messianic recipe that will endow design with shiny new attributes. When designers confuse style as somehow being equivalent to a theoretical concept, both theory and its embodiment in design suffers. Rather, each influences the other through indirect relationships. **Postmodern theory**, for example, **cannot be merely illustrated with layered or**

Zombie Modernism

It Lives!

This is a very scary essay. It's about death and denial. But you don't have to be afraid to read it, because it's just language, and meaning is arbitrary. At least that is what those nasty postmodernists and deconstructivists want you to believe. But we know better. There is a right way and a wrong way to do everything. A good way, and a bad way, a rational way and a crazy way, a clear way and a chaotic way, the modern way and the modern way. In graphic design, there is no alternative to modernism. To postdate modernism is to be a commercial artist, printer or scribe, not a designer, because the designer was born out of modernism. To postdate modernism is equally incomprehensible for most designers, because

Mr. Keedy

[17]

Continued on page 31.

Emigre no. 34, "Rebirth of Design"

Magazine spreads

EDITOR/DESIGNER Rudy VanderLans
PRINCIPAL TYPEFACES Arbitrary, Matrix, Keedy Sans, Dogma Outline
CLIENT Emigre Graphics

USA, 1995

In 1995, *Emigre* made an unexpected change to a smaller page size. While the revised format signalled a new emphasis on writing, the magazine's page structures are still subject to constant reinvention. Issue 34 (previous page) uses the visible grid structures of the later large-format issues to divide the page into horizontal bands so that three articles can proceed in parallel. The two "Mouthpiece" issues mount an examination of the relationship of writing and design with a fluidity unconstrained by the reduced format.

Emigre no. 35, "Mouthpiece" part 1

Magazine spreads for an article about clients

GUEST EDITOR	Anne Burdick
WRITER/DESIGNER	Denise Gonzales Crisp
ILLUSTRATOR	Tom Tierney
PRINCIPAL TYPEFACES	Triplex, Bembo, Caslon, Cooper Black, Berthold Script
CLIENT	Emigre Graphics

USA, 1995

Writingdesign **Designwriting**
by Louise **Sandhaus**

CLICK* CLICK

Exploding ideas about design

In the catalog for the Pop Art show that toured the U.S. a couple of years ago, there was an essay by cultural observer Dick Hebdige. In it he described the term "pop" not as the "pop" in "popular" but "pop," the textual onomatopoeia of the sound "pop." But "pop" is not much of a bang for something so seemingly loud and significant as the impact when one strikes the other world. But as we were talking about "click." Could this small, light blow be the sound of a big bang in digital space — the collision of the world of writing and the world of design?

This is an essay.

An essay explores ideas.[B-] This is an essay that explores the idea of the essay itself and what the essay might be in the context of computer-based publications. I would like to explore the idea of the examination of ideas given that the parameters for defining form and content become muted and indistinct in digital publishing environments.[~]

[B-] Just to be sure, I looked up "essay" in the dictionary, thinking that I would find a definition that had something to do with writing. To my surprise, the first definition of "essay" an attempt." It wasn't until the third definition that there was anything about writing at all, and this was a "concise" dictionary, not one of those 12 volume deals, so it had to get to the point quickly.

[~] I'm imagining something here beyond the garden variety periodical in our own digital present, where computer-based publications dot the electronic landscape like acts on a leftover Twinkie. For the most part, few are more than elaborate hyper-versions of print, only with a larger and more diverse network of links — not unlike footnotes found in print-based essays.

Emigre no. 36, "Mouthpiece" part 2

Magazine page and spread for an article about writing and design
GUEST EDITOR Anne Burdick
WRITER/DESIGNER Louise Sandhaus
PRINCIPAL TYPEFACES Clarendon, Letter Gothic
CLIENT Emigre Graphics

USA, 1995

These new environments are the collision of a variety of communications means (print, digital and telecommunicative), ways (words, images and sounds) and forms (stories, essays, drawings, music, etc.). (that are frequently associated with pleasure and entertainment.)

But primarily, we could describe digital environments as structured spaces that are visual, textual and aural. Each aspect draws on its own language to express and communicate.[~]

Designfully, we are artists who give shape to different types of information and ideas by utilizing different means, ways and forms. We work and play in the realms of meaning and the means by which meaning is made and carried, giving form to ideas and ideas to form. We make things comprehensible within a given context to a particular audience. And since we like to think of ourselves as something other than communications engineers, hopefully we charm and delight somewhere along the way.[~]

Combining the abilities of designers with the nature of electronic environments, where how something is said conveys ideas as much as what is said, it seems like just the right time, place and space for some explosive idea exploring. So, "[i]f the audience has changed, and the production has changed, and the messages might change, wouldn't common sense suggest that the notion of form might evolve too?"[~]

The difficulty with conceiving of a digitally-based essay as something other than text stuffed into 1s and 0s is that text is generally regarded as the standard bearer for conveying complex ideas. So we're talking about a considerable paradigm shift.[~]

"You know, it's a picture book. Needless to say, it doesn't have a lot of narrative urge."

Form + Zweck no. 2/3

Magazine spreads
DESIGNERS / Daniela Haufe, Detlef Fiedler
DESIGN COMPANY / Cyan
PRINCIPAL TYPEFACE / Bureau Grotesque
CLIENT / Form + Zweck

Germany, 1991

Published in Berlin, *Form + Zweck* addresses
design issues from a historical, practical
and theoretical perspective and its own
design reflects the critically informed
modernism of its editorial position. Cyan's
typography is extreme in its formalism yet
controlled with precision. Type and image
are engineered into mutually reinforcing
structures, while atmospheric photography,
sometimes reminiscent of the 1920s
avant-garde, is used to counterpoint the
textual arabesques. Colour and a high degree
of attention to the material qualities of
paper and binding play an essential role.

Form + Zweck no. 7/8

Magazine spreads
DESIGNERS | Daniela Haufe, Detlef Fiedler
DESIGN COMPANY | Cyan
PRINCIPAL TYPEFACE | Bureau Grotesque
CLIENT | Form + Zweck

Germany, 1993

Form + Zweck no. 9/10

Magazine spreads
DESIGNERS | Daniela Haufe, Detlef Fiedler
DESIGN COMPANY | Cyan
PRINCIPAL TYPEFACE | Bureau Grotesque
CLIENT | Form + Zweck

Germany, 1994

Form + Zweck no. 11/12

Magazine spreads
DESIGNERS Daniela Haufe, Detlef Fiedler
DESIGN COMPANY Cyan
PRINCIPAL TYPEFACE Bureau Grotesque
CLIENT Form + Zweck

Germany, 1995

The width of the margin s
of values or lack of ther
analysis book.

Now, said E, with refere
around wide margin w
cate sensibilities with
aloof from the multit
beauty and good tas

You are an island, E
across a vast gulf o

Zed no. 1, "The Politics of Design"

Journal cover and spreads
EDITOR/DESIGNER Katie Salen
PHOTOGRAPHERS Karen White, Sonya Mead, Katie Salen
PRINCIPAL TYPEFACES Interstate, Frutiger
CLIENT Center for Design Studies,
Communication Arts and Design,
Virginia Commonwealth University

USA, 1994

ows culture, aestheticism and a sense
, s/he said, quoting the handwriting

ce to your signs there, you have an all
ich shows a person of extremely deli-
ove of color and form, one who holds
de of lives in his own dream world of

aid, and I'm communicating with you,
darkness.

Ideas do, indeed, have consequences.

Nearly a year ago the concept for this journal was borne out of a perceived gap, or margin, in the current design dialogue. No forum
presently exists within the field of visual communications that deals with fundamental issues of
concern to practitioners, educators, and students
as a group, and acknowledges the impact of these
issues on society. It is true that there is a lot being
said—we are all speaking—but not to each other, it
seems. Divided by age, generation, ideology, and circum-
stance, designers, educators, and students have, in the
past, retired to common ground where the language and
concerns are familiar and where there is little chance of step-
ping off the edge. Consequently, designers speak to other designers, academics to other academics, and students to no one
in particular, or any who might listen.

And so the margins grow. We have wrapped our conversa-
tions tightly around ourselves, blankets of white noise offered with
expectations of sameness. Entrenched and faithful to our own cause
we have lost interest in the value of debate and of a community rich in
individual opinions and ideas. It is just easier that way.

Inevitably, the gap widens.

Editor's note

For better or for worse, design has entered a state of balkanization—now a sprawling,
fragmented borderland of communities turned inward, fiercely territorial and dismis-
sive of anything perceived as "other". Each holds up its philosophy for emulation
and grounding as the status quo—the way of being and seeing in the [design]
world. Assimilation is encouraged, even by those prizing subjectivity as a noble
pursuit - for it is us against them. Choose or move on.

This "either-or" mentality has designer, educator, and student alike pledg-
ing weary allegiance to an uncertain cause. How many times in recent history
have we found ourselves surfing the edge of the periphery while simultaneously emulating and rejecting the center? Expressivity or objectivity?
Theory or pragmatics? Modernism or Grunge? Maybe we are trying too
hard. Perhaps we needn't believe that the shared, or agreed upon, is
more valuable in our pursuit than difference and contradiction. History
should be enough to show that there are no absolutes. Our conscience
and aesthetic taste are, equally, products of the cultural environment
in which we grow and are educated. As Anne Burdick has written,
"What we require is a set of ideologies that accepts and analyzes
rather than disdains and dismisses." To this I would add an awareness of the self-defined value-system of our field and a respect
for the depth of intellectual and aesthetic experimentation
being pursued all around us, regardless of personal "taste".
**Each is an indelible part of the other, separate but connect-
ed through this activity we call design.**

In fostering the growing gap between theory and
practice, technology and craft, Modernism and everything
else, we are participating in our own special version of
capture-the-flag—that childhood game of power and
single-minded pursuit. One we/man, one flag. World
domination. We would do well to remember the day
as children when we grasped that four-square resulted in far fewer bruises and that in this game, the
bully was never hero.

To understand this, then, is to understand
what *Zed* is all about. To identify and embrace
the margins; to question, debate, and question
again; to weigh the alternatives and consider
the possibilities.

**Solidarity: Subversive Technologies
in the Production of Political Change**

Abstract

Diane Gromala

The Solidarity movement in Poland not only produced an enormous variety of design artifacts during the 1980's, but also developed elaborate and subversive networks of dissemination. Initially
the first independent trade union in an Eastern Bloc country, Solidarity operated, for the most part, as an underground social and
political movement. Characterized by nonviolent and subversive
resistance to a repressive Communist rule, it is credited with playing
an instrumental role in Poland's bid for self-determination. This
resulted, in 1989, in the first democratic elections held in a communist
country since 1946.

The production and distribution of design played a primary role
in the processes of the pluralistic mass movement of radical democratic
change. Instrumental in creating and reinforcing sites of contestation
and, to a lesser degree, negotiation among social, political, and economic
forces, it facilitated the efforts of an estimated <10> million Solidarity
members, or a majority of Poles, during the 1980's. The nature of design
produced and distributed by Solidarity in this specific context calls into
question commonly held assumptions of the ways in which design is understood in the West, particularly issues related to the relationships of technology, design, and cultural contexts.

giggly girlie

ideal

dumb blonde

Zed no. 2, "Real World Design:
The Role of the Experimental"

Journal cover and spreads
EDITOR/DESIGNER Katie Salen
PHOTOGRAPHERS Nancy Nowacek, Katie Salen
PRINCIPAL TYPEFACES Interstate, Myriad
CLIENT Center for Design Studies,
Communication Arts and Design,
Virginia Commonwealth University

USA, 1995

Zed is an annual publication that aims
to bridge the gap between designer, student
and teacher by acting as a vehicle for divergent
viewpoints and new voices. While conforming to
the conventions of the "design journal" in its booklike
proportions and editorial tone, *Zed* manifests a high
degree of purposeful experimentation in its design. In
the second issue, on the theme of the experimental, the
letter "i" is deleted from some articles, requiring readers to
"assimilate the unfamiliar" and adapt their method of reading
to the modified presentation.

12　13

Bulldozer no. 0

Spreads from a graphic design magazine
ART DIRECTOR/DESIGNER　Frédéric Bortolotti
DESIGN COMPANY　Bulldozer
PHOTOGRAPHERS　Daniel Pype, Simon Niedenthal
PRINCIPAL TYPEFACES　Arbitrary, Serifa, Blur, Garamond
CLIENT　Bulldozer

France, 1993-94

I like the

The most familiar "use" of vernacular is to produce nostalgia. The problem with the nostalgic vernacular is that it steals from the past to deny the future. The past is robbed of its authenticity and historical context (or specificity) to be rewritten as if it were an episode of *Happy Days* or a Norman Rockwell painting. Absence makes the heart grow fonder, and there's no fiction like "the good old days." This kind of nostalgic reverie is an escape from the anxiety of an uncertain future; it's not so much historical quotation as it is nostalgic sound bites. Authenticity is NOT a high priority for graphic designers because it's usually the feeling we're after, NOT the fact. This allows us to play fast and loose with history to construct feelings, like that of the art deco thirties or the fifties, that never really correspond to any specific time, place, or people. It's not the past, it's better than the past - and the present and the future. Retreating into nostalgia is turning your back on the present and running in fear of the future. If graphic designers are busy daydreaming about the good old days, then who is going to show us what the future looks like? Who's in charge of inventing tomorrow? Are we all so embarrassed that the modernist visions of Herbert Bayer, Raymond Loewy, and Bucky Fuller didn't exactly come true that we must retreat to some imaginary past life that didn't really exist, either?

The commercial artist was transformed into the graphic designer with the help and encouragement of modernism. Graphic design's identity is so codependent on modernism that one does not dare contemplate design outside of the modernist paradigm. Now, in an era of postmodern plurality and technological change, the good old days of the easy and unchallenged answers of modernism are gone for good. That's why graphic design is suffering from an identity crisis. When you are having trouble defining something it is often easier to define what it is NOT, and the vernacular is what we (professional graphic designers) are NOT.

I think much of the current interest in vernacular is a symptom of the lack of direction and grasping for self-definition of the design profession. So many times I hear designers waxing poetically about some lovely little matchbook cover, menu design, or hand-lettered sign and how terrific it is—what graphic designer doesn't have a stash of such found goodies to "borrow" from? And there's nothing wrong with that; after all, the capacity to appreciate something will expand your understanding, NOT define it.

vernacular

Appropriation of the "other" (to use the current art world vernacular) means taking something from a culture "other" than your own. You can appropriate something without reference to its original context (pastiche), or in a way that calls attention to it's original context (parody/irony). Other cultures are not just liberal's other cultures (the high, low, pop, and subcultures). When one culture borrows from another there are often anthropological or social traumas at both rance and equality. For example, when the high culture graphic designer (trained in a design school) borrows clip art/illustrations or crude lettering from low culture hack (trained in the school of hard knocks) it can be a condescending act of elitism that deliberately draws attention to the difference in status between them as if to say:

"Hey, look at what this so-called illustrator did...isn't it corny? I could never do anything that silly, I'm too sophisticated. I really wish I could but I'm just too clever to do anything like that. In fact, I'm too clever to do anything at all, that's why I have to use stuff from these poor hacks."

This appropriation/nostalgia thing has not only become a bit tiresome lately, but is increasingly mean spirited as well; but only in the most covert fashion because the plunderers are always the first to proclaim how much they love the one they are plundering. The idea of "borrowing" in graphic design is so pervasive that it's often done unconsciously. What is needed is an awareness of what crossing cultural/historical barriers actually means, as well as an understanding of the importance of context.

How many more graphic designers must pass the timeless undead visions of ... COMET VERNACULAR ?

The culture that is perceived to be high or dominant is not the only one to be empowered. In this negotiation of status, the plundered underdog is given the unassailable status of the authentic, capable of true, natural, or honest expression. The so designated dominant culture on the other hand envy or worship (or fear/misunderstanding the) TRUTH from the poor but happy. Thus, the once all dominance of the culture war is redistributed. They played "the great" but also "that they're main stream commercial" they're just "crap." In this exchange of bittertat, the high and low cultures are leveled out into one popculture. Is it the graphic designer's task to please everyone in this pan-pop culture? Or to affirm their client's status as the high, and the audience/consumer's status as the low?

You can't please some of the people some of the time, but you can please all of the people all of the time!

Today, cutting-edge vernacular users are the designers creating rave graphics. (For those of you who live in a cave, a rave is an illegal underground party of a thousand kids on ecstasy [DRUG] dancing in puddles of their own sweat to techno/house music until the cows come home, or the cops drop in [FUN].) The old and low cultures that rave designers borrow from are principally American corporate and package design of the seventies and eighties (now there's some hacks)! Rave designers love logos, lots of color, and outlined type; and hey, who doesn't? The fact that the "professional designer's" work is now being reworked like any other bit of ephemera might be some kind of poetic justice, but it fails to be a very interesting design strategy. That's because their work (like their predecessors) is essentially a one-liner that has little resonance beyond the "shock of the old." What little invention there is in rave graphics is provided mostly by the computer.

i remember the late 80s ... now those were the good old days!

At this point it would seem the vernacular idea in graphic design has pretty much played itself out. The only thing the cutting-edge appropriators can do is continuously reuse what they just did last year. This strategy couldn't really be called vernacular design, after all there are already a lot of designers who do this and call it "timeless design". Have you ever seen a dog chasing his own tail? Now that's timeless.

The past used to be considered a classic example or ideal for the present. In the postindustrial postmodern world the past is just another place to go shopping, except most of the past has been bought up, just leaving yesterday's news. Retrofitting a popular old song is the easiest way to get a hit. It is a very different thing to recycle the past for the purposes of "instant gratification" than to reinvent the past as an ideal for the present. Reinventing the past is a lot of hard work (scholarship), and who wants to wait for the future (it may never come). When the general cultural mood is here-today-gone-tomorrow, all history is reduced to one undifferentiated vernacular (no linear hierarchies, please).

Is there a "correct" way to use the idea of vernacular in graphic design, or is the whole idea of the vernacular overly simplistic and not very useful?

Isn't getting "inspiration" from your *Print, How, I.D.* and *Emigre* magazines using the vernacular?

Why is it that graphic design history includes cave painting, cuneiform alphabets, and woodblock engravings but doesn't include sign painting or clip art?

When is the vernacular just history?

What is the point of asking all these questions if you aren't going to answer them?

NOT!
by Mr. Keedy

Currently, graphic design practice and history is neither specific nor general in its scope; rather, it is obviously constructed out of fickle self-interest and unchallenged ego. Unchallenged, because for the most part the rest of the world doesn't give a shit about graphic design anyway.

Maybe we should either expand our notion of what constitutes graphic design or become even more specific and rigorous in our self-definition of graphic design practice. Maybe graphic designers should go back to the old business of inventing the future instead of regurgitating a past that's been digested so many times that it has no taste (not to mention style).

Deep down inside I think most designers suspect that "using vernacular" is a chicken shit's easy way out. It's a retreat from style, or at least from expressing your own style forged from your own experience and time. Graphic designers should be responsive to and responsible for the development of their own style. Instead of just "using" the vernacular we are creating it, and it tells us not only who we were and are, but who we hope to be

Lift and Separate: Graphic Design and the Quote Unquote Vernacular

Essay spreads from an exhibition catalogue

EDITOR | Barbara Glauber
WRITER/DESIGNER | Jeffery Keedy
PRINCIPAL TYPEFACE | Manu Sans

The monograph examines the complex relationship between the vernacular and the contemporary graphic designer. Ten essays explore the hierarchy, appropriation and recontextualisation of various visual dialects, including the use of nostalgic imagery and the graphic language of roadside signage. Most of the contributors are practising designers whose visual voices are expressed through the design of their articles.

Lift and Separate: Graphic Design and the Quote Unquote Vernacular

Essay spreads from an exhibition catalogue

EDITOR   Barbara Glauber
WRITER/DESIGNER   George LaRou
PRINCIPAL TYPEFACES   Egyptian, Gill Sans, Boy Wide
CLIENT   The Herb Lubalin Study Center, The Cooper Union

USA, 1993

Coil no. 1

Cover and spreads from a
journal of the moving image

DESIGNER Damian Jaques

DESIGN COMPANY Proboscis

PRINCIPAL TYPEFACES Wunderlich, Quadraat,
Disturbance, Coventry, OCRB

CLIENT Coil

Great Britain, 1995

the poetics of blue

Helene Cixous, in "Manna", describes the battered world of the exile as the "celestial tariff"...

"Blue is a film one watches with more than one's eyes.

Coil is an independent publication that addresses the cultural, theoretical and practical aspects of the moving image (film, video and digital/electronic imaging). The contrasting natures and thematic concerns of the different media are reflected in a design which asks for a high degree of involvement from the reader. Early feedback suggests practitioners feel the time is right for a journal presenting this subject matter in a highly activated visual style.

psi net
Kathleen Rogers

the perpetual minute
Wayne Stretch

Rebecca Horn began documenting her performances on Super 8 in 1970 with "Einhorn" (Unicorn) and on 16 mm film in 1972 (Performances I), and, by natural extension, completed her first feature-length film, "Der Eintänzer", in 1978. Her keen interest in the life and work of silent film maker and actor Buster Keaton has been widely analysed, but here I wish to ascertain her affinities and interests with film as a medium, as an appendage to her activities and interests and which has influenced her work in other media.

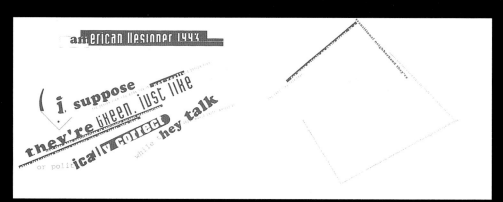

In this celebratory catalogue the ambiguous nature of the creative process is given the same emphasis as the clarity of the designers' philosophies and finished work. The book is structured and paced to reflect the range of rhythms the viewer would experience in exploring the exhibition. Subtle differences between elements and dramatic juxtapositions suggest the eclectic nature of American design.

Art of Design 2

Spreads from an exhibition catalogue

DESIGNER Susan Lally

DESIGN COMPANY Lally Design

PRINCIPAL TYPEFACES Futura, Goudy, Franklin Gothic, Garamond

CLIENT Harry Wirth and the American Design Network

USA, 1993

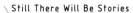

Still There Will Be Stories

Children's illustration exhibition poster/catalogue
DESIGNER Carlo Tartaglia
ILLUSTRATORS James Jarvis, Sara Fanelli
PRINCIPAL TYPEFACE Univers
CLIENT Royal College of Art

Great Britain, 1994

Cut and folded, the poster also
functions as a catalogue. Text is
used as digitally manipulated texture
on the cover, reversing the usual
relationship between word and image
in conventional children's story books.

BIS Publishers, Amsterdam   ISBN 90-72007-19-0   Printed in the Netherlands

NED.

Architecten

volume 1

---

register
index

263

---

architecten
architects

Book spreads

DESIGNERS Jacques Koeweiden, Paul Postma
DESIGN COMPANY Koeweiden Postma Associates
PHOTOGRAPHER Marc van Praag
PRINCIPAL TYPEFACES KP DIN, Stone
CLIENT Uitgeverij BIS

The Netherlands, 1994

voorwoord
preface

inleiding
introduction

Architectonische kwaliteit en
het belang van referenties
Architectural quality and the
importance of references
dr. ir. H. de Vroom

Het bouwproces
The building process
Olof Koekebakker

Problems and Solutions:
Surveying the Work of Jon Tower

Exhibition catalogue cover and spreads

DESIGNERS Laura Lacy-Sholly, James Sholly
DESIGN COMPANY Antenna
PRINCIPAL TYPEFACES Clarendon, Bell Gothic, STA Portable
CLIENT Herron Gallery, Indianapolis Center
for Contemporary Art

USA, 1992

Jon Tower's art deals with the
processes of socialisation that shape
perceptions of religion, education, art
and science. The catalogue represents
the conceptual nature of his work by
distilling elements from the visual
culture of these disciplines into a
document that is part laboratory
report, part text book and part early
volume on art.

Black Maria no. 2

Magazine cover (front and back)
DESIGNER Cornel Windlin
PRINCIPAL TYPEFACE Custom-made for the project
CLIENT Black Maria

Switzerland, 1994

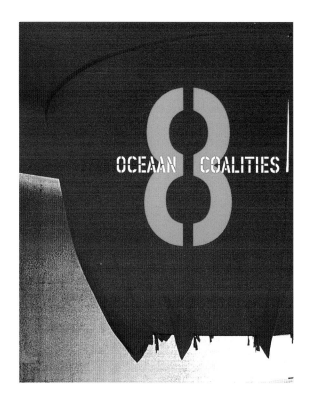

Oceaan Coalities

Catalogue cover and spreads
DESIGNER Roelof Mulder
DESIGN COMPANY Roelof Mulder Studio
PHOTOGRAPHERS Jozee Brouwer, Christa van Kolfschoten
PRINCIPAL TYPEFACE Ocean Normal
CLIENT Oceaan Galerie

The Netherlands, 1992

OCEAAN

COALITIE IS EEN TENTOONSTELLINGSPROJEKT DAT IN 1991 IN OCEAAN
PLAATSVOND. TWEE INITIATIEFNEMERS VAN OCEAAN, HESTER OERLEMANS EN
NIEK DE JONG BESLOTEN HUN EIGEN KUNSTENAARSCHAP ALS UITGANGSPUNT TE
NEMEN VOOR EEN SERIE TENTOONSTELLINGEN. KUNSTENAARS WERDEN
UITGENODIGD EEN INHOUDELIJK VERBOND MET ÉÉN VAN HEN AAN TE GAAN OM
ZO GEZAMENLIJK TENTOONSTELLINGEN TE REALISEREN.
DE TENTOONSTELLINGEN DUURDEN STEEDS DRIE WEKEN EN WERDEN
AFGEWISSELD MET ZOGENAAMDE 'ZATERDAGAVONDTENTOONSTELLINGEN'
WAARIN JUIST DOOR KUNSTENAARS INGEDIENDE PLANNEN CENTRAAL STONDEN.
AAN DE 8 COALITIE-TENTOONSTELLINGEN DIE IN OCEAAN HEBBEN
PLAATSGEVONDEN HEBBEN MEER DAN 25 KUNSTENAARS DEELGENOMEN.
DAARBIJ ZIJN DE MEEST UITEENLOPENDE DISCIPLINES, ZOALS DESIGN,
FOTOGRAFIE, GRAFIEK, SCHILDERKUNST, PERFORMANCE, ARCHITECTUUR,
SCULPTUUR, TECHNIEK EN KERAMIEK TE ZIEN GEWEEST.
COALITIE HEEFT EEN BIJZONDERE REEKS TENTOONSTELLINGEN OPGELEVERD
WAARMEE OCEAAN HAAR HEEL EIGEN VISIE OP HET BEGRIP
'KUNSTENAARSINITIATIEF' HEEFT KUNNEN LATEN ZIEN.

COALITIES

BORN TO BE WILD

COALITIE IS EEN COMMUNICATIEPROGRAMMA. TWEE OF MEER KUNSTENAARS GAAN VOOR EEN BEPAALDE TIJD MET ELKAAR IN ZEE EN PROBEREN EEN VERBINDING TUSSEN HUN WERK TOT STAND TE BRENGEN. EEN GESPREK OP ARTISTIEK-INHOUDELIJK NIVEAU MET EEN TENTOONSTELLING ALS RESULTAAT. EEN JAAR LANG HEB IK IEDERE DRIE MAANDEN EEN TENTOONSTELLING GEMAAKT STEEDS IN SAMENWERKING MET ÉÉN OF MEERDERE KUNSTENAARS. ALS KUNSTENAAR NIEK DE JONG ÉN ALS ORGANISATOR. EEN BROEIERIGE DUBBELROL.

MET COALITIE WERD DE RELATIE TUSSEN ORGANISATIE EN KUNSTENAAR TOT EEN MAXIMALE INTENSIVITEIT OPGEVOERD. IK VOND HET NIET MEER ZO INTERESSANT OM VANAF DE ZIJLIJN TOE TE KIJKEN HOE COLLEGAE HET ER IN DE RUIMTE VAN ONS INITIATIEF VANAF BRACHTEN. MIJN IDEALEN REIKTEN VERDER DAN HET SLIJTEN VAN MIJN TIJD ACHTER HET BURO, DE TELEFOON EN DE COMPUTER. IK BEN IN DE WIEG GELEGD VOOR HET KUNSTENAARSCHAP ZELF. DAARBIJ GALERIES ZIJN ER GENOEG, HET WARE KUNSTENAARSINITIATIEF WORDT STEEDS ZELDZAMER. IK BEDOEL EEN PLEK WAAR GEÏNVESTEERD WORDT IN DE ONTWIKKELING VAN KUNSTENAARS. EEN PLEK DIE NIET ALLEEN MAAR OP ZOEK IS NAAR 'NAMEN', MAAR EEN VERANTWOORDELIJKHEID DRAAGT VOOR EEN ACHTERBAN. EEN PLEK DIE GEEN VOORWAARDEN STELT, MAAR ZE JUIST SCHEPT.

HET BELANGRIJKSTE DOEL VAN COALITIE WAS HET MAKEN VAN PRACHTIGE KUNST, DIT VOOROP. DAARBIJ DE MANIER WAAROP.
IK VERBAASDE ME ER LAATST OVER WAAROM IK VANAF HET BEGIN VAN OCEAAN OP ÉÉN OF ANDERE MANIER ALTIJD OP ZOEK WAS NAAR DIALOOG, NAAR EEN

KLANKBORD. IK VOND HET MAAR NIKS OM IN MIJN ATELIER AAN DINGEN TE WERKEN DIE GEEN DIREKTE FUNKTIE HADDEN, OM ALLEEN MAAR EEN BEETJE IN MIJN EIGEN GEDACHTENWERELDJE TE ZITTEN WROETEN. IK WILDE NAAR BUITEN MET HET SPUL, ZIEN WAT ER GEBEURT ALS JE MENSEN ERMEE KONFRONTEERT. OM JE ALS AANKOMEND KUNSTENAAR DOELEN TE KUNNEN STELLEN MOET JE EERST WETEN WIE JE BENT EN WAAR JE STAAT. OM DAAR ACHTER TE KOMEN MOET JE JE VERHOUDEN MET JE OMGEVING, COLLEGAE EN PUBLIEK, MET DE REALITEIT. EERST IS HET NATUURLIJK MOEILIJK OM DIE DIALOOG OP GANG TE BRENGEN. TOCH BLIJFT HET VOLGENS MIJ VAN LEVENSBELANG OM HET DAARNA OP GANG TE HOUDEN. DE KUNST MOET ZICH STEEDS BLIJVEN VERHOUDEN MET DE REALITEIT. EN IK DENK DAT HET DAAR NOG WEL EENS AAN SCHORT. VEELSTEVEEL MOOIE PLAATJES EN MOOIE PRAATJES.

HET WAS DE BEDOELING VAN COALITIE OM KUNSTENAARS UIT TE DAGEN. HOEVER KUN JE IN EEN SAMENWERKING GAAN ZONDER JEZELF TE BUITEN TE GAAN? KUN JE JEZELF WEL TE BUITEN GAAN? MIJN UITGANGSPUNT WAS NIET TE SNEL BIJ ELKAAR TE WILLEN KOMEN MAAR DE STRIJD JUIST OP TE VOEREN, DAAR HEB JE VEEL MEER AAN. KIJKEN TOT HOEVER JE KUNT GAAN. OP ZOEK NAAR JE GRENS. PROBEREN MEZELF EN DEGENE WAARMEE IK WERKTE TE DWINGEN TOT EEN ZO EXTREEM MOGELIJKE UITSPRAAK TE KOMEN.

DE ENE SAMENWERKING IS NATUURLIJK ANDERS DAN DE ANDERE. DE ENE IS OOK VEEL SPANNENDER ALS DE ANDERE. DIT GELDT VOOR COALITIE MAAR EIGENLIJK VOOR ELKE TENTOONSTELLING IN OCEAAN. STEEDS MOET IK PLAATSBEPALEN. WELKE ROL KAN IK BINNEN DIT GEHEEL SPELEN. SOMS LIJKT HET OF IK MIJN KUNSTENAARSCHAP BUITEN DE DEUR MOET ZETTEN EN SOMS IS MIJN

1E COALITIE
27 MAART

ZO WAS HET

VOOR DEZE TENTOONSTELLING HEEFT NIEK DE JONG DEAN BRANNAGAN UIT LONDEN UITGENODIGD NAAR ARNHEM TE KOMEN OM SAMEN AAN EEN TENTOONSTELLING TE WERKEN.
BRANNAGAN WERKTE VEEL MET HET BEGRIP ENGAGEMENT. ENGAGEMENT IS VERLOVING, EEN VERBINTENIS, MAAR OOK BETROKKENHEID BIJ MAATSCHAPPELIJKE ONTWIKKELINGEN. BRANNAGAN WAS ZEER GEÏNTERESSEERD IN DE GESCHIEDENIS VAN ARNHEM TIJDENS DE TWEEDE WERELDOORLOG. GEZAMENLIJK HEBBEN ZIJ EEN AANTAL HISTORISCHE PLEKKEN IN ARNHEM EN OMGEVING BEZOCHT. AL WERKEND ONTSTOND VANUIT DEZE ERVARINGEN EEN PERFORMANCE.
DE PERFORMANCE IS EEN REACTIE OP DE MANIER WAAROP DE GESCHIEDENIS HET VERLEDEN, DIE OP DE BEZOCHTE PLEKKEN NOG HEEL STERK VOELBAAR IS, INTERPRETEERT. ZO WAS HET (NIET).
HET PUBLIEK KOMT BINNEN IN EEN LEGE RUIMTE, NIEK DE JONG EN DEAN BRANNAGAN VOLGEN, BEIDEN IN HET ZWART GEKLEED. NIEK DOOPT EEN KWAST IN EEN EMMER DODEKOPVERF EN BEGINT LEVENSGROTE LETTERS OP DE MUUR TE KALKEN. DEAN ONTROLT INMIDDELS DE BRANDSLANG VAN OCEAAN. HIJ VOLGT DE VORM VAN DE LETTERS MET DE BRANDSPUIT. UITEINDELIJK WORDT DE ZIN 'ZO WAS HET' EVEN LEESBAAR OM HET VOLGENDE MOMENT ONZICHTBAAR TE VERDWIJNEN, DOOR EEN HARDE WATERSTRAAL UITGEWIST.

/STone UTTERS

Spreads from a book about John Baskerville
WRITER/DESIGNER Phil Baines
PRINCIPAL TYPEFACES Monotype Baskerville, Grot

Self-published
Great Britain, 1992

The ENGLISH form o ress, a n is

f seriffed, varied-weight (stressed) letter, t he norm to which the vernacular form gr avitates unless there is a good reason for it to resist, has a rich full shape, a vertical st nd a fairly sharp gradation from thick to thi n strokes; although it is less abrupt than in the characteristic French form. The differe nce of weight between strokes thick and thi often quite marked; the latter are virtually hairlines. R ich bracketted serifs terminate sharply, if not always a ctually to a point. The tails of the

Q & R

Apart from the work o f some of t he later W est Countr y tombston e carvers, t he vernacu lar traditio n

usually have great ver ve, the tail of the latt er being bowed, not st raight. Proportions te nd to be squarer and more regular than tho se of Roman forms. A, (p.9

The

The ENGLISH letter rance in 1754 when th writing master and ja *e* began producing his : although there can b signs were based on st eveloped by tombston irty years previously. T ans and **grotesques dense smoke of th tion round about 1** he first definitive form racteristics which now lish could be found in ms of early tombstone dates on houses, and e derived though they w ls.

W hether Bask erville was a cquainted w ith the 'rom ain du roi' it is imposs ible to say, but it is ne arly impossible that h e was not acquainted with Shelley's book: it is inconceivable that a ny professional writin g-master in the time Baskerville was teachi ng writing would not have known of the bo ok. And again, the let

ters

n has been little influe nced by ty pe designs. Indeed, th e influence has often b een very m uch the ot her way ro und. A, p.7

(T he 'romain du roi' was cut by Gra ndjean for the exclusive use of th e Royal Printing Hou se in France, it was fir st used to print *Medail les sur les Principaux Ev enements du Regne-de-Lo uis le Grand* in 1702. The type certainly is a

break

made its official appea e printer, lettercutter, panner *John Baskervill* innovative letterforms e no doubt that his de yles which had been d e carvers twenty or th he clarendons, egypti **emerged from the e Industrial Revolu 800.** But long before t s appeared, many cha seem particularly Eng the primitive letterfor s, builders' marks and ven in Caslon's types, ere from Dutch mode A, p.10

M uch - *I* think too much - h as been mad e of the writ ing masters' influence upon the tombstone c arvers. Probably the fi rst relevant master w as Cocker, whose spec imens were published around 1670; and fro m 1680 to 1741 hardl y a year passed witho ut other masters issui ng specimens. A, p.32

Amongst

Part history and part homage, the book explores John Baskerville's place in the English lettering tradition. The grid structure alludes to gravestones and rubbings but is used differently from page to page to express the subject matter.

ave endeavoured to produce a *Sett of Types* according to what I conceived to be their true proportion. D

The general brilliance ville's influenced e gns: as

Basker was th desi w mas

of
types
by
copybook
he himself
a writing

Their
however
far more
to those

ter. forms elate osely und on tombston es.

actual r cl fo

With generous curves, strongly differentiated thicks and th ins, long untapered but bracketted serifs, his types were fo llowed in 1769 by what is known today as *Fry's Baskerville* , (…).
A, p. 11

I f he had merely imi tated Caslon, even if he had improved on hi m, there would have b een little to say, or to s

peculate

F inally, after ma ny delays cause d by the desire of Baskerville t o have the book perfe ct, the Virgil went to press in 1757, after sev en years of careful, pa tient, persistent work upon it. It was a surp

rise

---

peculate about; but he bandoned a] the Caslon tradition, and with G randjean, F ourn ier a nd other type-cutters, began a new tradition which, in the eighte enth

rise to the literary wo rld. It was the first fi ne book printed in En gland. (…) Every part of the volume was in harmony with every o ther part. There was n o dissproportion. The book has been well sa id to be a landmark in the history of typogra phy. In looking at it t oday we wonder how it was done when it w as done. It seems as th ough the Birmingham artist had come befor e his time.   E, p.39

enth c e marts

ntury revo lutionised the appear ance of the printed pa ge. (…)

er appearance. (…) He pulled the thickest part of a curved letter away from the positio n of being 45° to the h orizontal and raised i t higher up the curve. (…) He made more of the serifs of the letters, m aking them more noti ceable by giving them a sharper, spiky quali ty. (…) These minute changes of detail would proba bly have gone unnotic ed (…) if it had not bee n for his

The revolution which Grandjean and Basker ville brought about w as in the relationship between the thick an d thin parts of a letter , in the position of th e thickest parts of the letter, and in the trea tment of the serifs. Al l these are minutiae; b ut type design is a ma tter of minutiae. Bask erville thickened the t hick parts of his roma n letter and made the thin parts thinner, giv ing them a sharper, s

sup erb p r e

He had a const ant succession o f hot plates of copper ready, b

etween which, a s soon as printed (…) the sheets w ere inserted. The wet was th us expelle d, the ink s et, and a g lossy surface p rut on all simu ltaneously.
E, p.65

s w o r k

superior ink, and s mooth paper.

Baskerville made o ther innovations in design. The type of th e late seventeenth cen tury was, on the whol e, rather compressed —whether for reasons of aesthetic appeal or economy it is difficult to say—but Baskervill e gave his letters a ro unded, open appeara nce. They take up a l ot of room.   B, p.161

T he type was cu t for him by Jo hn Handy (d.1 792) who, by t he time of Baskerville 's death, had worked

for

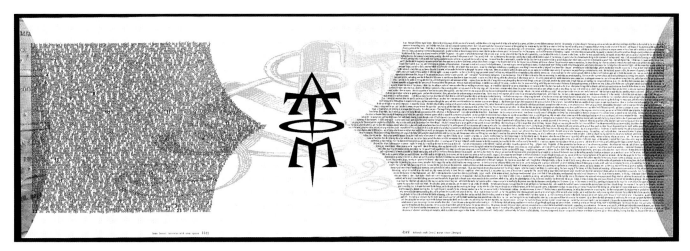

Semiotext(e) Architecture

Book spreads
EDITOR/DESIGNER / Hraztan Zeitlian
DESIGNERS / Reverb Struere, Margo Chase, David Carson, Barry Deck
CLIENT / *Semiotext(e)*

USA, 1992

DETERRITORIALIZED.

The large-format edition of the theoretical journal *Semiotext(e)* devoted to architecture achieved instant notoriety on its publication. Editor and project designer Hraztan Zeitlian enlisted a cast of American designers known for their experimental approaches to typography to construct a demandingly visual, not to say overloaded, examination of theory's role in architectural design.

Interference John Holden

ISBN No. 0-9523640-0-X

Published by
UMRAN PROJECTS 1994
£25

Distributed by
Cornerhouse Publications
70 Oxford Street Manchester
M1 5NH England
T 061 237 9662 F 061 236 7323

Gritty Typographics by Chris Ashworth
Text by Sean Cubitt
Design Assistance by David Smith
AJS I MAN F JH & Co.

Contact
Invisible T 071 284 7882

Book. Poster. Postcard.

Interference

Book spreads
DESIGNERS | Chris Ashworth, Neil Fletcher, Amanda Sissons, John Holden
PHOTOGRAPHER | John Holden
PRINCIPAL TYPEFACES | Custom-made for the project
CLIENT | Ümran Projects

Great Britain, 1994

Interference is a photographic essay on surveillance in the city. In response to John Holden's lushly sinister images, the designers created typographic illustrations of technological

Mmm ... Skyscraper I Love You

Spreads from a typographic journal of New York

WRITERS/DESIGNERS   John Warwicker, Karl Hyde
DESIGN COMPANY   Tomato
PRINCIPAL TYPEFACES   Compacta, Clarendon, Bureau Grotesque, Shelley
CLIENT   Booth-Clibborn Editions

Great Britain, 1994

Randomly spliced together, the pages of *Skyscraper* record the sights, sounds, "crosstalk and chaos" of a journey through the streets of New York. Material was first developed during the recording of Underworld's album *dubnobasswithmyheadman* (two of the group, including Karl Hyde, are members of Tomato). Subsequently published, the project is closely related to the artist's book genre, except that it is available in ordinary bookshops.

Olyan teljesen átlagos reggel, ami
egyszerre ígér mindent és semmit. Megpróbáltam felállni, de lábaim kifáradva a
nagy rohanástól meg-megbicsaklottak. Elvergődtem a fürdőszobáig, ráültem a
WC-re. 6 óra volt. Lassan agyamról felszállt a
köd, és ahogy minden reggel, felrajzolódott előttem az

új nap

összes teendőivel.

Rettenetesen elfáradtam. Reggel volt.

Le-ma-radt, le-ma-radt, le-ma-radt, le-ma-radt

Emlékszem, ahogy kidagadtak az
ereim, a hátamról csurgott a víz... Potty potty. Óraként csöppentek
le államról a kis sós cseppek.

Ujjaim nyújtózkodtak, kezem
mint középkori kínpadon, egyre nőtt.
A vonat azonban érzéketlenül táncolt,

mindig pár centivel előttem.

üvöltötte egy
kegyetlen hang belülről. Egy kéz fehér lappal takarta le a tájat
és az eget, a vonat képe egyre egyszerűsödött a szemem előtt. Sziluettjét mintha
fekete ceruzával vagy tussal húzták volna át. Nem volt ott már más, csak a
száguldozó monstrum és egy absztrakt fájó rohanás. Ez azonban kínjaimon nem
enyhített és a feladat sem tűnt értelmetlenebbnek. A lényegen nem változtathat
semmi, amikor az ember tudja, hogy rohannia kell, mert lemarad.

Rövidülni Kezdet

Spreads from a literary booklet
DESIGNER | Zsolt Czakó
WRITER | Krisztina Somogyi
PRINCIPAL TYPEFACE | Template Gothic

Self-published
Hungary, 1995

PERSPECTIVES on LOS ANGELES: *Narratives, Images, History*

**THE GETTY CENTER FOR THE HISTORY OF
ART AND THE HUMANITIES**
1996–1997
SCHOLARS AND SEMINARS PROGRAM

The Getty Center for the History of Art and the Humanities is dedicated to advanced research in the history of art, broadly defined as an integral part of human history and society. The goal of the Center is to cross the traditional boundaries imposed on academic institutions by bringing together international scholars to reexamine the meaning of art and artifacts and to reassess their importance within the full scope of the humanities and social sciences.

The Center's 1996–1997 Scholars and Seminars Program, *Perspectives on Los Angeles: Narratives, Images, History*, will be dedicated to research on Los Angeles and Southern California. Potential areas for exploration within this context include not only traditional forms of artistic and cultural expression, such as painting, sculpture, and architecture, but also journalism, photography, film, literature, the book arts, performance, urban studies, and all forms of popular and mass culture—each viewed in relationship to the ecologies, historical conditions, communities, and institutions that have affected its development. Research is understood in broad and inclusive terms that embrace the pursuits of scholars, artists, and cultural workers.

The Center solicits research proposals on all aspects of the artistic, cultural, social, economic, and political history of Los Angeles. Candidates may apply as Predoctoral or Postdoctoral Fellows, Getty Scholars, or Visiting Scholars. To receive an Application Packet with a detailed description of the Center's 1996–1997 scholar year, please contact your department administrator or:

THE SCHOLARS AND SEMINARS PROGRAM
THE GETTY CENTER FOR THE HISTORY OF ART AND THE HUMANITIES
401 Wilshire Blvd., Ste. 700, Santa Monica, CA 90401-1455, USA

(310) 458-9811, ext. 6000 *telephone*
(310) 395-1515 *facsimile*
Fellowships@getty.edu *e-mail*

Perspectives on Los Angeles: Narratives, Images, History

Poster
DESIGNER | Lisa Nugent
DESIGN COMPANY | ReVerb
PHOTOGRAPHER | Dennis Keeley
PRINCIPAL TYPEFACES | Alternate Gothic, Scala Sans
CLIENT | The Getty Center for the History of Art and the Humanities

USA, 1995

The Getty Center's 1996-97 Scholars and Seminars Program was dedicated to research on Los Angeles and Southern California. ReVerb's brief, for a poster to be displayed primarily at educational institutions, was to represent LA and its diverse cultures. The photographs compare two urban landscapes: a freeway system and a caged animal. The typography reinforces the visual language of the photography by mimicking the barriers and screens as well as the organic.

Dysmedia

Self-promotional video
DESIGNER Barry Deck
EDITOR AND EXTRA SHOOTING Uwe Wiesemann
PRINCIPAL TYPEFACES Truth, Cyberotica

USA/Germany, 1995

Born/Burn: Paper + Cathode

Exhibition poster
DESIGNER / P. Scott Makela
DESIGN COMPANY / Words and Pictures for Business and Culture
PHOTOGRAPHER / Billy Phelps
PRINCIPAL TYPEFACES / Officina, VAG Rounded, Trade Gothic, WAC Mittelschrift
CLIENT / Kendall College of Art and Design

USA, 1995

National Portfolio Day 1992

Poster inviting prospective students to show their work
DESIGNER/PHOTOGRAPHER/ILLUSTRATOR | Alexei Tylevich
PRINCIPAL TYPEFACES | Blur, Template Gothic, custom-made for the project
CLIENT | Minneapolis College of Art and Design

USA, 1992

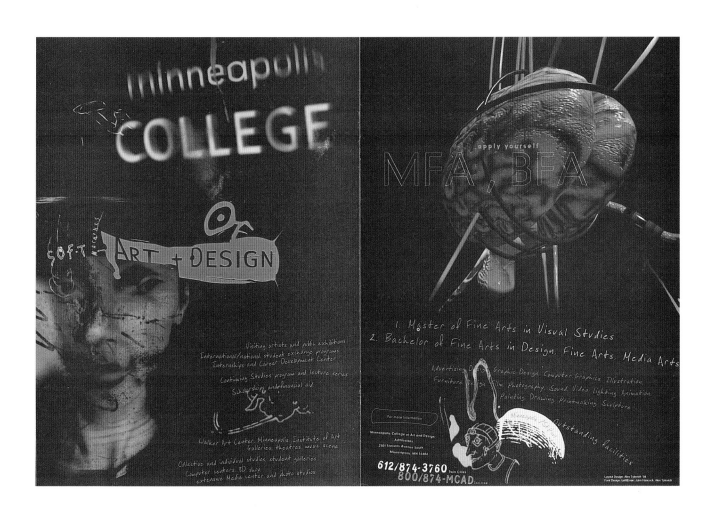

Magazine advertisement aimed at high school advisers and students

DESIGNER/ILLUSTRATOR / Alexei Tylevich

PRINCIPAL TYPEFACES / Calculus, Hancock, Stamp Gothic

CLIENT / Minneapolis College of Art and Design

USA, 1993

Alexei Tylevich's poster for the Fourth
International Symposium on Electronic
Art expresses the contemporary merging
of art, technology and the body as a
brutal "cyborg icon" – an anonymous,
wired, Christlike figure immersed in fluid
tissue, through which the type itself
seems to course like a new kind of
informational blood.

FISEA '93

Conference poster
DESIGNER/PHOTOGRAPHER/ILLUSTRATOR Alexei Tylevich
PRINCIPAL TYPEFACE Custom-made for the project
CLIENT Minneapolis College of Art and Design,
International Symposium on Electronic Art

USA, 1993

Exhibition poster
DESIGNER/ILLUSTRATOR Alexei Tylevich
PRINCIPAL TYPEFACE Custom-made for the project
CLIENT Minneapolis College of Art and Design

USA, 1994

1 2 3 4 5 6 7 8 9 5

9 8 7 6 5 4 3 2 1 0

INTERDISCIPLINARY ARTS FELLOWSHIP S

INTERMEDIA FELLOWSHIP MCKNIGHT

AZANDE, RICARDO BLOCH,
LAURIE BETH CLARK, DAVID DUNLAP,
WENDY MORRIS

and music? Can a found object be sculpture? And the relevant question for critics and viewers often seemed to be "Yes, but is it ART?"

Interdisciplinary Fellowships 1994

Catalogue
DESIGNER | Jan Jancourt
DESIGN COMPANY | Jancourt & Associates
PHOTOGRAPHER | Warwick Green
PRINCIPAL TYPEFACES | Franklin Gothic, Officina
CLIENT | Intermedia Arts

USA, 1994

Conceptually, the poster/brochure uses a number of "texts" or "voices" to create a dialogue with the reader. Since the graphic design programme's philosophy is divided into three frameworks (cognitive interaction, cultural dynamics, information media environments), three images were chosen to represent these areas. The only proviso was that they should all relate to the statement "I found myself against a wall, when it hit me like a ton of bricks", intended to suggest the student's moments of frustration and discovery.

Master of Graphic Design Recruitment

Poster/brochure
DESIGNER/PHOTOGRAPHER | Andrew Blauvelt
PRINCIPAL TYPEFACES | Bell Gothic, Trade Gothic, Letter Gothic
CLIENT | Department of Graphic Design,
North Carolina State University

USA, 1995

ATLANTA COLLEGE OF ART GALLERY

WITH NEO-CONSERVATIVES ONCE AGAIN TRYING TO TAKE THE UPPER HAND IN THE CULTURAL REALM,

OUTSIDE
the Basic Curriculum
Redefining Education
and Artistic Practice

A SYMPOSIUM
SATURDAY, APRIL 1, 1995

Based on a TV image of US Speaker of the
House Newt Gingrich, whose controversial
history course was broadcast by satellite, the
poster announces a symposium on the ways
educators and artists can begin to counteract
the political advances made by America's right
wing, which now defines the agenda on cultural
issues. The designers scanned in a copy of the
standardised handwriting model for students
("the Basic Curriculum") but let the program's
outline recognition software redefine their
shapes according to its parameters.

Outside the Basic Curriculum:
Redefining Education and Artistic Practice

Conference poster
DESIGNERS   Andrew Blauvelt, Anne Burdick
PHOTOGRAPHER   Anne Burdick
PRINCIPAL TYPEFACES   Monospace 821, DIN Neuzeit Grotesk, Manuscript
CLIENT   Atlanta College of Art Gallery

USA, 1995

OPEN HOUSE AT ART CENTEF
SUNDAY, APRIL 4, 1993

11:00 a.m.-4:00 p.m Explore the campus
See student work and talk with faculty in the area of your choice:
Advertising, Environmental Design, Film, Fine Art, Illustration, Industrial
Design, Graphic and Packaging Design, and Photography.
12:00 Welcome Address
1:30 Admissions Seminar
2:30 Financial Aid Seminar
3:30 Admissions Seminar (repeat)

Art Center offers B.F.A., B.S., M.F.A., and M.S. degrees.
Applications are accepted for summer, fall, and spring semesters.
For more information on the Open House, call the Admissions Office at 818.584.5035
Art Center College of Design 1700 Lida Street Pasadena, California 91103.
See the back of this poster for a map to Art Center.

Art Center inside/out

	Open House at Art Center
	Poster
DESIGN DIRECTOR	Rebeca Méndez
DESIGNERS	Rebeca Méndez, Darin Beaman
DESIGN COMPANY	Art Center College of Design
PHOTOGRAPHER	Steven A. Heller
PRINCIPAL TYPEFACE	Franklin Gothic
CLIENT	Art Center College of Design
	USA, 1993

Refuel; replenish fuel supply. **Refuge;** place of shelter from pursuit, danger or trouble. **Refugee;** taking refuge, especially in foreign environment, from persecution, war or disaster. **Refuse;** convey by action that one will not submit or consent. **Refuse;** what is rejected as worthless or leftover after use. **Re-fuse;** to fuse again, blend or amalgamate into one.

Refuel, Refuge, Refugee, Refuse

Exhibition poster
DESIGNER Joan Dobkin
DESIGN COMPANY Joan Dobkin Design
VIDEO STILLS Gadi Gofbarg
PRINCIPAL TYPEFACE Franklin Gothic
CLIENT Seigfred Gallery, School of Art, Ohio University

USA, 1993

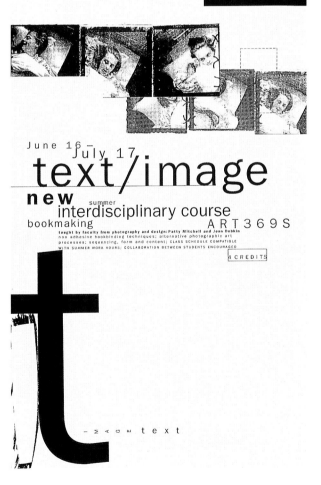

Text/Image

Promotional poster for a new course offered by the faculties of Design and Photography
DESIGNER Joan Dobkin
DESIGN COMPANY Joan Dobkin Design
PHOTOGRAPHER Patty Mitchell
PRINCIPAL TYPEFACE Franklin Gothic
CLIENT School of Art, Ohio University

USA, 1993

de Program 1992

Poster
DESIGNER/PHOTOGRAPHER Doug Kisor
PRINCIPAL TYPEFACE City
CLIENT Eastern Michigan University Design Department

USA, 1992

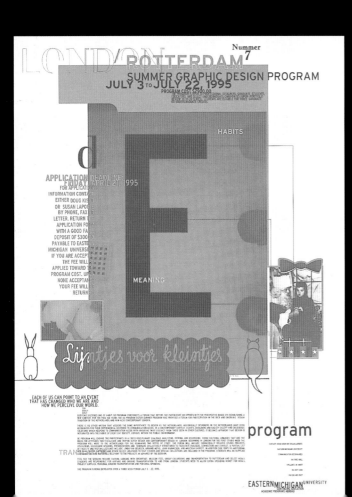

Doug Kisor's posters promoting European study programmes for American designers offer complex visual analogues of their educational intentions. Their aim is to model potentially life-changing experiences in ways that suggest the intellectual "layering" that is central to the programmes' approach. The 1992 poster addresses Dutch notions of the "modern" within the context of early 1990s design debates.

London/Rotterdam Design Program

Poster
DESIGNER/PHOTOGRAPHER Doug Kisor
PRINCIPAL TYPEFACES Interstate, One Iota
CLIENT Eastern Michigan University Design Department

USA, 1995

de Program 1994

Poster
DESIGNER/PHOTOGRAPHER Doug Kisor
PRINCIPAL TYPEFACE Industry
CLIENT Eastern Michigan University Design Department
USA, 1994

Otis College of Art and Design 93-94/94-95

Fold-out cover and catalogue spreads
DESIGNERS Lisa Nugent, Whitney Lowe, Somi Kim
DESIGN COMPANY ReVerb
PHOTOGRAPHER Dennis Keeley
PRINCIPAL TYPEFACES Clarendon, Steile Futura, Script
CLIENT Otis College of Art and Design

USA, 1993

ILLUSTRATION
GRAPHIC DESIGN

GRAPHIC DESIGN
ENVIRONMENTAL ARTS
FASHION

"Better the rudest work that tells a story or records a fact, than the richest without meaning."

47

John Ruskin THE SEVEN LAMPS OF ARCHITECTURE (1849)

"The important task of all art is to destroy the static equilibrium by establishing a dynamic one.

Piet Mondrian in CIRCLE (1937)

The catalogue's theme, "set things in motion", is expressed through the use of shifting type and flowing, banner-inspired shapes. The density of type and image is intended to reflect the energy of campus activity.

ENVIRONMENTAL DESIGN

Patricia Belton Oliver

PATRICIA BELTON OLIVER
CHAIR, ENVIRONMENTAL DESIGN DEPARTMENT

"In the Environmental Design
Department, we endeavor to
teach habits of mind—curiosity,
wonder, open-mindedness, and the
capacity to think critically and creatively—
which enable an understanding of process
and the interconnectedness of things, and an ability to
suspend judgment, which becomes useful in designing in new situations.
Ours is an educational structure that relies on interactions and interdependencies that are
dynamic and consequently promote flexibility, which is essential to the process of
learning. We believe in binding, not bounding."

ENVIRONMENTAL DESIGN

Art Center College of Design Catalog 1995-96

Catalogue spreads

DESIGN DIRECTOR Rebeca Méndez

DESIGNER Darin Beaman

ASSOCIATE DESIGNER Chris Haaga

PHOTOGRAPHER Steven A. Heller

PRINCIPAL TYPEFACES Perpetua, Minion, Franklin Gothic, Helvetica, Tema Cantante, Lip

CLIENT Art Center College of Design

USA, 1994

California Institute of the Arts

CalArts

Cover and spreads from California Institute of the Arts catalogue, 1995-97
DESIGNERS Somi Kim, Barbara Glauber
DESIGN COMPANIES ReVerb, Heavy Meta
PHOTOGRAPHERS Steven A. Gunther, Paula Riff, Raymond Hahn, Stephen Callis
PRINCIPAL TYPEFACES Arbitrary, Jot, One Iota, OutWest, Platelet, Tribulation, Wormwood
CLIENT California Institute of the Arts

USA, 1994

ART
THEATRE
FILM/VIDEO
MUSIC
DANCE
School of CRITICAL STUDIES

13
portfolio

31 schools
72
48 THEATRE
ART
42
FILM/VIDEO
MUSIC
CRITICAL STUDIES
DANCE
50

This is a school of film and video makers—
the tool may be a camera, an optical printer or computer.
Any path the moving image has taken in the past
or might take in the future is kept open for exploration and use.
Since enthusiasm underlies all creative and imaginative
production, we welcome highly motivated students
with an independent and daring approach towards their discipline.
● We offer an education based on comprehensively designed and tested curricula
with a strong emphasis on artistic and intellectual boldness.
The courses, classes and workshops combine practical training in skills and craftsmanship
with theoretical inquiry. Working and production progress in
constant dialogue with aesthetic reflection and critical thinking.
● The Live Action program establishes a laboratory for innovative, unconventional forms of experimental, narrative and documentary film and video making. Experimental Animation and Character Animation, both internationally renowned programs, nourish individual development as well as the technical facility of their students. Joint computer labs provide facilities in these areas that keep pace with advancing technologies. ● The interschool program Directing for Theatre, Video and Cinema (offered in partnership with the School of Theatre) furnishes young directors and actors with fundamentals upon which they can rely in their future profession. ● To produce vivid and vigorous works of art, student film and video makers need an inspiring exchange with their colleagues, teachers and mentors. To shape, deepen and enrich their visions, the School relies on three interdependent assets: a body of curious, courageous, and challenging students with a critical power of judgment and ingenuity; an outstanding faculty with exemplary workmanship freely sharing their experience and knowledge; and an inventory of equipment, facilities and machinery which is continually renewed and upgraded. ● One factor which makes CalArts special is the presence of different arts in one setting. Students can benefit from this prolific contiguity, and for this reason we urge them to take courses in the disciplines of other Schools and to participate in all the activities and potentials the Institute provides. As the saying goes: someone who knows nothing but chemistry, doesn't know it well at all.

SCHOOL OF

film/
video

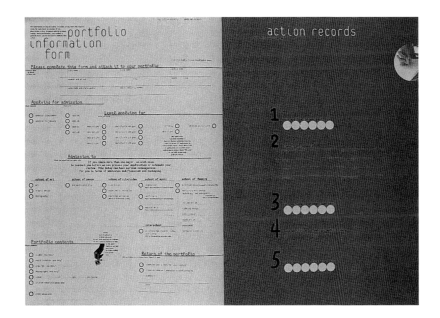

portfolio
information
form

action records

Flyer for a lecture by Edward Fella
DESIGNER Edward Fella
PRINCIPAL TYPEFACES By Fella's CalArts students
CLIENT Art Center College of Design

USA, 1995

Flyer for a lecture by Mike Fink
DESIGNER Edward Fella
PRINCIPAL TYPEFACE OutWest
CLIENT Graphic Design Program, California Institute of the Arts

USA, 1993

Edward Fella's lecture "announcements" are made, with some perversity, long after the event itself is over. As with his earlier Detroit Focus Gallery series, their defiantly non-digital, hand-lettered inventions refer not to the visiting artists and designers (except in the case of his own lectures) but to Fella's pet themes and predilections. The poster for graphic designer Mike Fink featuring Fella's typeface OutWest takes its cue from another historical "Miche Phinck", who in the early 1800s earned a wild west reputation as a brawler, braggart and marksman.

Central Department
Michigan of
7 p.m., University
Thursday Art Students in design
March 2, 1995
142 Wightman Hall present:

for
Edward;
Fella,
Freework
in time!

Flyer for a lecture by Edward Fella
DESIGNER Edward Fella
PRINCIPAL TYPEFACES Custom-made for the project, Cooper Black
CLIENT Central Michigan University Department of Art

USA, 1995

Flyer for a lecture by Nick Bell

DESIGNER / Edward Fella
PRINCIPAL TYPEFACES / Custom-made for the project
CLIENT / Graphic Design Program, California Institute of the Arts

USA, 1994

164

Flyer for a lecture by Rebeca Méndez
DESIGNER | Edward Fella
PRINCIPAL TYPEFACES | Custom-made for the project
CLIENT | Graphic Design Program, California Institute of the Arts

USA, 1993

Flyer for a lecture by Neville Brody
DESIGNER | Edward Fella
PRINCIPAL TYPEFACES | Peter Regular, Marsha Demi, Greg Bold,
Jan Ultra, Cindy Light, Bobby Italic
CLIENT | Graphic Design Program, California Institute of the Arts

USA, 1994

Winter
1994

Errant

Bodies

Errant Bodies

Cultural journal cover
DESIGNER Louise Sandhaus
PRINCIPAL TYPEFACES OutWest, Walbaum
CLIENT Brandon LaBelle

USA, 1994

Errant Bodies

Cultural journal cover
DESIGNER Louise Sandhaus
PRINCIPAL TYPEFACES Suburban, Monoline Script, Grotesque
CLIENT Brandon LaBelle, Louise Sandhaus

USA, 1994

Errant
Bodies
Winter 94/95 *Spring*

Good stuff inside!

Poster for a literary reading
DESIGNER Brian Schorn
DESIGN COMPANY ReVerb
PRINCIPAL TYPEFACES Letraset Sourcebook, Gill Sans

Self-published
USA, 1993

robert blake's
*surreal
vision*

h. turnip smith
*the phone call
(disgustingly funny)*

the funding game
*free expression
and a slash of cash*

USA $3.95
Canada $4.95
vol. 2
no. 3

Surreal vol. 2 no. 3

Arts magazine cover
DESIGNER | Brian Schorn
PRINCIPAL TYPEFACES | Harting, Madrid, Onyx, Blackoak, Kaufmann
CLIENT | *Surreal*

USA, 1994

USA $4.95
Canada $5.95
vol. 2 no. 2

BRANKA
BOGDANOV
marries art & video

COMICS:
underrated
political
stirring

*Beautiful as the chance encounter
on a dissecting table of a sewing machine
and an umbrella.
—Lautréamont*

Surreal vol. 2 no. 2

Arts magazine cover
DESIGNER | Brian Schorn
PRINCIPAL TYPEFACES | Harting, Madrid, Technocrat, Shelley
CLIENT | *Surreal*

USA, 1994

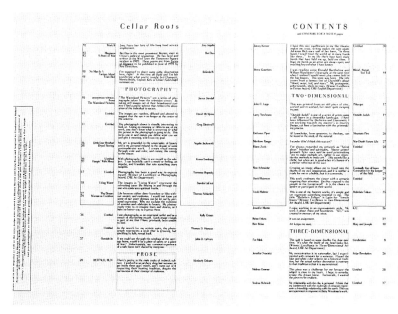

The 1994 *Cellar Roots* was designed as a response to conservative criticism of the design of previous issues. The golden mean, the Arts and Crafts movement and nuances found in letterpress were used as references and the typefaces Flattop and Procession also contain a historical reference to the structure and proportions of Bodoni. The satirical aim was to produce a "beautiful magazine" to showcase the art and literature department's work.

Cellar Roots

Cover and spreads from a magazine
of literary and visual arts

FACULTY ADVISER — George LaRou
DESIGNERS — Craig Steen, Sharon Marson
DESIGN COMPANY — Eastern Michigan University Design Department
PRINCIPAL TYPEFACES — Flattop, Procession
CLIENT — Eastern Michigan University Student Media

USA, 1994

Cellar Roots

Cover and spreads from a magazine
of literary and visual arts
FACULTY ADVISER George LaRou
DESIGNERS Anne Bourselth, Kindra Murphy, Kevin Sams, Andy Slopsema, Lori Young
DESIGN COMPANY Eastern Michigan University Design Department
PRINCIPAL TYPEFACES Celly, Starlight
CLIENT Eastern Michigan University Student Media

USA, 1995

Dress Like the Boss

	Poster
DESIGNER	Elliott Peter Earls
DESIGN COMPANY	The Apollo Program
PRINCIPAL TYPEFACE	Helvetica
	Self-published
	USA, 1993

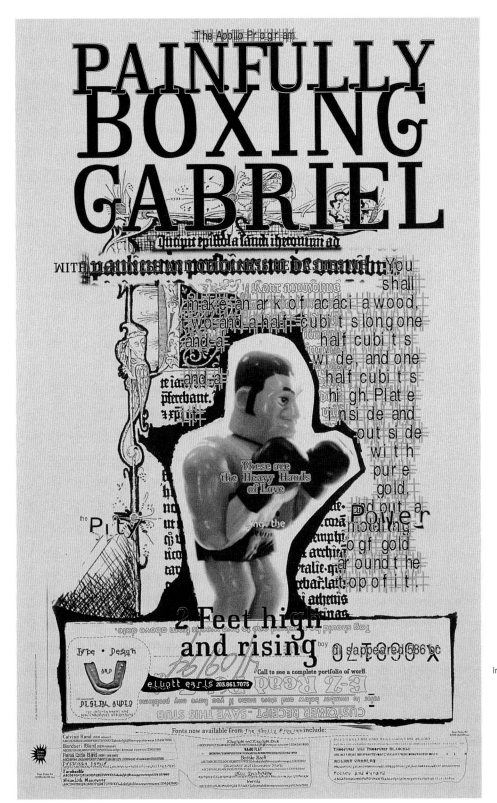

Painfully Boxing Gabriel

Poster
DESIGNER Elliott Peter Earls
DESIGN COMPANY The Apollo Program
PHOTOGRAPHER The Apollo Program
PRINCIPAL TYPEFACES Calvino Hand, Bland Serif Bland

Self-published
USA, 1995

In his self-published posters, often designed to promote his own typefaces, Elliott Peter Earls poses fundamental questions about experimental design. "How do we restore radicality to the creative process when pluralism renders all work valid and no work taboo?" he asks. "How can we deal with the pervasive 'legitimation of the subversive'?" Earls's personal answer is the literary concept of defamiliarisation. With his bizarre typography he makes the familiar strange and the strange familiar and in the process questions the viewer's assumptions about "form" itself.

Dysphasia, Dysplasia, Dyslexia

Poster advertising three typefaces

DESIGNER | Elliott Peter Earls
DESIGN COMPANY | The Apollo Program
PHOTOGRAPHER | The Apollo Program
PRINCIPAL TYPEFACES | Dysphasia, Dysplasia, Dyslexia

Self-published
USA, 1995

The Conversion of Saint Paul

Poster
DESIGNER / Elliott Peter Earls
DESIGN COMPANY / The Apollo Program
PHOTOGRAPHER / The Apollo Program
PRINCIPAL TYPEFACES / Mothra Paralax, Toohey, Wynand

Self-published
USA, 1995

No. 3
1993
$15

Now Time no. 3

Cover and contents spread from a magazine of social and cultural criticism

DESIGNERS	Somi Kim, Whitney Lowe, Susan Parr, Lorraine Wild, Caryn Aono, Andrea Fella
DESIGN COMPANY	ReVerb
ILLUSTRATOR	Michael Greco
PRINCIPAL TYPEFACES	Antique Olive, Souvenir
CLIENT	A.R.T. Press

USA, 1993

Now Time is sponsored, in part, by the generosity of individuals who are interested in supporting art and culture in Los Angeles through a forum which allows for a wide diversity of voices from people working to free the Human Spirit!

All contributions to Now Time are tax deductible to the full extent of the law. Friends of Now Time will join our masthead and will be invited to our special events. Please make out your check to Art Resources Transfer, Inc., earmarked "Now Time."

$24 Subscriber
$100 Friend
$250 Friend
$500 Friend
$1000 Friend

Contents:

Interviews

Essays

New writing

Script Excerpts

Project pages

Art

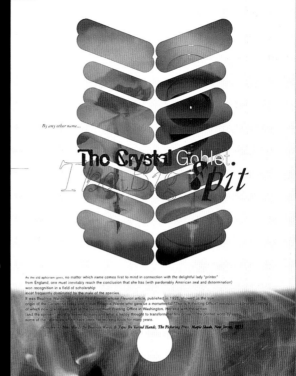

By any other name...

The Crystal Goblet.
The Big Spit

As the old aphorism goes, no matter which name comes first to mind in connection with the delightful lady "printer" from England, one must inevitably reach the conclusion that she has (with pardonably American zeal and determination) won recognition in a field of scholarship most frequently dominated by the male of the species.

It was Beatrice Warde (née Becker) whose *Fleuron* article, published in 1926, showed as the true origin of the Garamond types. It was Beatrice Warde who gave us a monumental "The U.S Printing Office" inscription—a bronze casting of which now graces that office in the Government Printing Office in Washington. Her skill with the written (and the spoken) word as served to many and what a happy thought to transform her fine prose to the printed word by using some of the typefaces which have been her working tools for many years.

Concerning Some Words By Beatrice Warde, & Types By Varied Hands, The Pickering Press, Maple Shade, New Jersey, 1955

The Crystal Goblet.The Big Spit

Pages from a visual essay published in the promotion
Rethinking Design II: The Future of Print

DESIGNER | Allen Hori
EDITORS | Michael Bierut, Emily Hayes
DESIGN COMPANY | Bates Hori
PHOTOGRAPHERS | Christopher Weil, Allen Hori
PRINCIPAL TYPEFACES | Akzidenz Grotesk, Melior, Garamond
CLIENT | Mohawk Paper Mills

USA, 1995

Imagine that you have before you a flagon of wine.
You may choose your own favorite vintage for this imaginary demonstration, so that it may be a shimmering crimson in color.
You have two goblets before you.
One is of solid gold, wrought in the most exquisite patterns.
The other is of crystal-clear glass, thin as a bubble, and as transparent. Pour and drink; and according to your choice of goblet, I shall know whether or not you are a connoisseur of wine. For if you have no feelings about wine one way or the other, you will want the sensation of drinking the stuff out of a vessel that may have cost ten thousand dollars; but if you are a number of that vanishing tribe, the amateurs of fine vintages, you will choose the crystal, because everything about it is

everything about it is
*calcula*ted ...her than hide the bea...ful thing which it was meant to contain.

hello

...long-winded and fragrant meta... ...es of the perfect wine-glass are ... ...m that obviates fingerprints on the ... ...between your eyes and the fiery heart o... margins on the book pages similarly meant to obviate the necess... type-page? Again: the glass is colorless or at the most only faintl... *Beatrice Warde* bowl, because the connoisseur judges wine partly by its c... impatient of anything that alters it. There are a thousand manners, typography that are as impudent and arbitrary as putting port in tu... green glass! When a goblet has a base that looks too small for securit... matter how cleverly it is weighted; you feel nervous lest it should tip... are ways of setting lines of type which may work well enough, and yet k...

Fluxus Vivus

Poster for a month-long Fluxus festival
DESIGNERS/DIGITAL IMAGING Rick Valicenti, Mark Rattlin
DESIGN COMPANY Thirst
PRINCIPAL TYPEFACES News Gothic, random video grabs
CLIENT Arts Club of Chicago

USA, 1993

A House Swarming!

Pages from a poem/foreword for a journal of literature and art

DESIGNER/PHOTOGRAPHER | Stephen Farrell
WRITER | D. R. Heiniger
PRINCIPAL TYPEFACES | Beach Savage, Werkman Round, Evangelic, typewriter
CLIENT | *Private Arts*

USA, 1994

Fire at J. D. Salinger's House

Unpublished poetry promotion/font specimen poster

DESIGNER   Stephen Farrell
WRITER   Daniel X. O'Neil
PRINCIPAL TYPEFACE Tetsuo Organic

USA, 1993

Stephen Farrell's pieces with the poet
Daniel X. O'Neil are rare but highly
suggestive examples of close creative
collaboration between designer and
writer. In *Injured Child*, text and
typeface illustrate each other. Both
are commentaries on brokenness: the
poem on the broken social and political
structures of Europe, the typefaces –
Farrell's own designs – on the fractured
nature of communication in English.

Injured Child Flown to London

Limited edition print
DESIGNER/ILLUSTRATOR Stephen Farrell
WRITER Daniel X. O'Neil
PRINCIPAL TYPEFACES Entropy, Commonworld, Stamp Gothic

Self-published
USA, 1994

ALTHOUGH THE COMPUTER AIDS IN
CERTAIN DESIGN TASKS, MUCH AS THE
TECHNOLOGY OF LASERS AIDS THE
SURGEON, ULTIMATELY THE HAND AND
EYE ARE THE PRIMARY TOOLS.

TYPE BECOMES A SPECIMEN, NOT
ON THE SHEET, BUT ON THE
OPERATING TABLE. LETTERS CAN
NOW BE EXPLORED AS LIVING,
ORGANIC WONDERS BY REMOVING
OLD TISSUES, TRANSPLANTING NEW
ORGANS, OR GRAFTING NEW LIMBS.

THE RESULTANT FORMS, SOMETIMES
CURIOUS ANOMALIES, SOMETIMES
FLORAL BEAUTIES, INEVITABLY
CHALLENGE THE CONCEPTION OF
TYPOGRAPHY TODAY.

BRIAN SCHORN

TYPOGRAPHY

IN THE INTERACTIVE WORLD IS FLUID, AND BOTH THE

TEXT AND THE DESIGN

CAN BE OPEN TO

RE-INTERPRETATION & RE-CONFIGURATION

BY THE

READER/USER.

THE OPTIONS MAY EXIST AS VARIABLES CREATED BY THE

AUTHOR/DESIGNER,

OR DESIGN MAY BE ALLOWED TO ROAM FREE, OPEN TO

CROSS-FERTILIZATION.

MICHAEL WORTHINGTON

THE DOMINANT AND REPRESSIVE ROLE OF THE TEXT OVER THE IMAGE IS BREAKING DOWN. AS THE DESIRE TO FIX IMAGE CONNOTATION IS REPLACED BY A MORE INCLUSIVE AND OPEN UNDERSTANDING, THE BOUNDARIES BETWEEN WORDS, SOUNDS AND IMAGES DISSOLVE INTO THE ELECTRONIC FLOW.

JEFFERY KEEDY

student

The book brings language and literature by way of the visual word to our eyes. We have **symbols** for the sounds of which the word is composed.

the book exists as an extension of the eye and mind but requires an understanding of the **code** of reading, and the mental participation of the reader to recreate the reality it is depicting.

Paradox: in order to be able to manifest itself concretely, language must first become *abstract*

A book piles up letters only for the ☐ ☐ ☐ ☐ ☐ of their arrangement - you have to know 2 ☐ ☐ ☐ ☐ ☐, that of the language and that of the letters.

No human society can exist without communication. We rely on signals, symbols of what we think and feel and want, and these signals can assume a vast variety of forms. We can wave our hands, screw up our faces, shrug our shoulders, use semaphore, telephone, morse code, run a pirate radio transmitter, or stick pins in dolls but will always end up with human speech as the most subtle, comprehensive, and exact system of communication we possess. Without speech, and the various notations of speech, human society would not be possible at all.

Human speech is essentially a system of conventional signs, though theorists once held that all language came out of a desire to imitate natural phenomena. There are, in all languages, many words which attempt an image of the things they represent; for example 'splash' sounds like water, 'pop' like the bursting of a balloon. Even with purely visual images, it is possible to find a certain appositeness in the form of the words. For example, the word 'moon', in Latin and its derivatives, as well as Russian, has a lun-form, and Malay has 'bulan'. It is the u-sound which is descriptive; the lips have to imitate a moon shape in order to give the right quality to the tongue sound; the back of the tongue is raised high, very close to the palate, and this seems to suggest that the moon is something high up. A word like 'little' seems apt, for the i-sound is made by narrowing the passage between the front of the tongue and the palate, suggesting that only something very little could creep through.

But this class of iconic words is very small. Structural words like 'of', 'if', 'when', 'so' - have never had a corresponding image in the outside world. Language is arbitrary, conventional, and has been so from the beginning.

An alphabet is a series of signs representing signs. The sounds making up a word stand for something in the outside world, and the letters which make up the word represent that sound. Thus, with a visual system of representation, we are two removes from reality. We are three removes from reality when we use a system like braille or morse; the dots and dashes or embossed letters stand for alphabetic letters; the alphabetic letters stand for sounds; the sounds stand for what exists in the mind or in the outside world.

abstract

The earliest attempts to represent the word by visual signs, were iconic. Chinese symbols still show ancient attempts to draw the referent (the thing in the outside world which the sound represents) of the word, and, when this direct representation failed, to use metaphor for rendering the abstract concrete. Egyptian picture-writing is full of recognisable lions, gods, snakes and birds. Our own alphabet is ultimately derived from hieroglyphics, but all picture elements have disappeared: the essence of the alphabet method is its conventionality. Only in the letter O, which seems to have come from an Egyptian drawing of an eye, do we find anything approaching an iconic purpose; where the letter represents the shape of the mouth when pronouncing the O sound.

Anthony Burgess

symbols

The form that the thought takes is that of language. Our language is a code that we agree to interpret, a system of communication. Our language shapes, and is shaped by, our perception of the world around us. It is so powerful that we cannot think without it.

The Magazine of the Book

Magazine spreads presenting research from the project "When is a book not a book?"
DESIGNERS Vivienne Cherry, Seònaid MacKay
PRINCIPAL TYPEFACES Custom-made for the project

Royal College of Art
Great Britain, 1995

words

arc prisoners

within the
book

each because

of the pages
is perceived
at a different
moment in time
a book
is a sequence
of
spaces in

A book contains secrets,
that can only be
discovered when the
book is opened.

secrets

reading that are intrinsic to the work

form determines conditions of

The book by its nature as an object subject to a progressive process of unfolding of that which is seen or yet to be seen the does not itself, is at once

reveal   **conceal** of decoding (reading) and

future pages themselves until, by the action turning pages, they

when its most successful space modifies communication imposes

A book

The book has its own space time structure by the very nature of its physicality; holding information that is revealed at a given moment.   The form of the book takes you from beginning to end, but the author decides where these points are and the nature of the journey in between.

invitation to follow the path
book, when we accept its
in the world of the
deliberate isolation
The darkness is our
towards its end.
definition - progressing
it is a story or a
the narrative whether
The path is of course
a surrounding darkness.
a path of light in
hand and lead us on
a book. Books take our
starts the moment we open
one-to-one experience that
nowhere and the
labels. That is however
everywhere, posted signs.
It is true that we read

chaos

Anything that escapes our systems of numbering
or ordering, or which cannot
fit into the categories of 'before', 'now'
or 'after' is seen as chaos.

Sequentiality is inherent to the structure of the book. Language and letters are lined up in strings of code, waiting to be read in turn, to lead the   reader towards future rows. This linear progression moulds all that we can see and understand. In French the word 'sense' also means 'direction'.

for things to make sense they must have direction

the order of sequence   **sense**

TETRACYCLINE

ASPARTAME

STEROIDS

PEROXIDE

FREON

MTV

SILICON

Chemicals needed in order to be a truly modern person.

Douglas Coupland · Shampoo Planet · Published by Simon and Schuster

Chemicals
Venice Beach
Grandpa

Poster project based on Douglas Coupland's novel *Shampoo Planet*

DESIGNER Martin Carty
PRINCIPAL TYPEFACES Custom-made for the project

Royal College of Art
Great Britain, 1995

Fast Forward

Book documenting a series of lectures and
projects about graphic design in the computer era

ART DIRECTOR | Jeffery Keedy
DESIGNERS | James Stoecker (front), Margo Johnson (back)
PRINCIPAL TYPEFACES | Keedy Sans, VAG Rounded

California Institute of the Arts
USA, 1993

sample d wild
t ext

St art Anywhere

text Eric Martin

A digital object is always alive, never finished.
In dividual authorship becomes problematic.
The "common document" becomes the norm.
There is no "original," every copy is identical to
the first created.

Fast Forward

Essay spreads

DIRECTOR | Jeffery Keedy
WRITERS | Lorraine Wild, Eric Martin, Jeffery Keedy
DESIGNERS | Shawn Mckinney, Shelley Stepp, Scott Saltsman
TYPEFACES | Keedy Sans, VAG Rounded

California Institute of the Arts
USA, 1993

In this short self-published book,
the vernacular type of the computer
keyboard is juxtaposed with banal imagery
to question the nature of binary touch and
our relationship with digital technology. Is
escape from this seductive environment
possible? asks the designer.
Who controls whom?

MIN/MAX

Book pages
WRITER/DESIGNER   Liisa Salonen
PRINCIPAL TYPEFACES   OCRA, Ariston, Trade Gothic,
Peignot

Cranbrook Academy of Art
USA, 1995

Systems

Poster/mailer
DESIGNER/PHOTOGRAPHER Jeremy Francis Mende
PRINCIPAL TYPEFACE Univers

*Cranbrook Academy of Art
USA, 1994*

The self-published poster discusses
cultural and individual fragmentation
and the contemporary schizophrenia of
identity and memory. The piece invites
viewer response via a mail-back card so
that both emotional and analytical
information can be re-entered into the
creative process, thereby evolving it.

And the body-vehicle,

moving across the landscape,

interpreting, re-interpreting,

feeds its conclusions

back into itself. Evolving.

Each cycle spins a thread,

stringing displaced fragme

into a subjective sequence.

Each of us, with our questions

ties the past and the future

to our present.

re-input

questions
become milestones
pathways:
nodes in a mental landscape.
Superhighways re-introducing a continuity of language, object, image, and place.
A mapwork of common states of mind.

and flickering between moments
phasing in and out of time-incremental, I
ask a question

ideal   real

part
st staccato moments
//instances//

occupying the whole
field of vision

nonlinear
image of
place

.how
much
time
is
left.

goes.

sharp
fragment of time
amplified and intense

Bridges
among
water.

because it is   //now//

folks straggling along vast stretches of concrete,
heading into the plane.

Even the words floating in air make blue shadows.

| APPROVED BY : | | DRAWN BY |
| | | REVISED |

Hey guess what? What? I've learned how to talk. Great.

| | | DRAWING NUMBER |

the person whose head
was incomplete burst into tears.

rience itself. Please re-input the perceived product.

We are involved in the initial swell of the **fourth wave** in the evolution of communication.

The first wave was spoken language, which initiated formal communication. Written language, the second wave, enabled people to keep a record of what they said and thought and did. The third wave, the printing press, revolutionized communication by making information and ideas accessible to the masses. And now the fourth wave, digital communication, the instantaneous transmission of ideas and information across space as nothing more than a series of 1s and 0s, is changing communication methods.

By asking ourselves these key questions, we can begin to realize the possibilities and different needs of the digital medium.

Faced with the task of building new constructs for this digital communication, we need to ask ourselves how do we write, design and orchestrate for multimedia. How do we create interfaces that are expressive and intuitive? What specific considerations are there when designing for multimedia that are different from designing for print? And, finally, how do we react to the shift in emphasis from author (*non-interactive messages*) to user? (*interactive, editable information*)

Multimedia environments are experiential places where the message is perceived as much as conveyed. Much like a conversation, the information is conveyed on a multitude of levels. This is one of the fundamental differences between print design and multimedia design.

However, *interface design*, for the most part, has *is to multimedia* treated the digital environment as merely a point and click novelty. Much of the interface design that exists today was designed by non-designers: programmers, game-makers and other visually uninformed developers. The result is digital environments that borrow heavily from the constructs of books, with interactivity being limited to clicking an ugly button with type on it, or hypertext links that leave little to the imagination. **Most "interactive" design is about as exciting an experience as programming your VCR.**

Designers today, because of our Postmodern education, have a blurry and yet expanded definition of what it is to be a designer. The lines between artist, graphic designer, animator, illustrator, photographer, and interface designer are less rigid. As a result, we can move freely between mediums, further blurring the line between design (*traditionally a language of commercialism*) and art. (*self-authorship of form and message*)

Fortunately, our design experience working with image, type, form and language makes us ideal candidates to create intuitive, expressive interfaces.

And considering that an interface is to multimedia what the horse is to the cart, it is a good place to begin.

As with print design, the message finds its expression in how it looks and how it feels. But in the digital medium, the expressive nature of the design also benefits from how it sounds, moves and behaves. In a sense, the information, comes to life and interacts with the viewer.

So how come, then, *America On-Line* is so offensively clunky and non-expressive with its flat graphics and simple planes of information? It's because the designers (or programmers, more likely) failed to think of the possibilities of digital media. They used the construct of time to get you from point A to points beyond, but each screen is still limited 2-dimensionally, like pages torn from a book and linked. And what little "design" there is is limited to stereotypical stylistic representations or "graphics" at the top of those screens. For instance, the travel section has a blurry image of a jet lifting off with bad curly-60s cursive type.

For all their attempts to distinguish the sections (or pages), it ends up looking the same.

Each page is treated in the same neutral and vague way. The viewer has no sense, after a while, exactly where they are within the AOL world. Ironically, it's like a drive through the suburbs where the onslaught of strip malls and fast food joints becomes numbing.

And America On-Line is not alone, *E-World* Apple's evolution of interface design, is guilty of much of the same short-sightedness. Sure it improves on AOL by creating a (somewhat) navigable environment, but once you get a layer or two beyond this world the interface reverts to the same old book/page construct.

What is missing is an interface that takes advantage of all the senses of multimedia: expressiveness through typography, imagery, sound and space. *Don't surprise me; don't offend me.*

Print is Dead! is the research portion of an interactive sound and motion project exploring experimental interface design. It seeks to discover what qualities make for a fluid, intuitive interface, what aspects of existing interfaces should be built on or scrapped, and how navigation through digital spaces can become more customisable and expressive. Deliberately crude and purposefully arcane in appearance, the hand-printed book is intended to have a charm and tactility that most multimedia experiences presently lack.

Print is Dead! Or so it seems

Spreads from a thesis project

WRITER/DESIGNER — Richard Shanks
PRINCIPAL TYPEFACES — Cooper Black, Suburban

California Institute of the Arts
USA, 1995

would consider how we perceive and access information and create an expressive representation of that.

For instance, what **expressive qualities** should a travel section have that a financial section shouldn't, and vice versa?

What clues could a designer provide for the viewer that create a **sense of place** within as large and varied a space as an online service?

How could the **navigable items** —the buttons, hypertext links and section heads—be redesigned to have their own constructs

based upon today's technology and communication methods, rather than those borrowed from print?

As I see it, there are four basic **types of interfaces**: the first being **hypertext**, where words in one story are "hot" or linked to other texts, the second is the traditional **button/menu** environment that we've all seen a million times; third, which is slowly becoming popular with E-World or Microsoft's Bob (big, bad Bob?) , is a spatial "hot" space with **metaphorical representations** of objects used in place of buttons.

The fourth type of interface is actually a combination of the above three types. It comprises a **navigable read map** with many different paths of exploration. Accessing this type of space more closely resembles a drive through the city— your own needs for accessing the space fuse with a sense of adventure.

Options of exploration (**leaps&links**) could be presented as they develop, rather than a button/menu environment which reveals (**leaps, links and edits— oh, my!**) its choices and depth (or lack thereof) all at once.

With a book, information is presented in a linear fashion. The reader is meant to read left to right, front to back. In multimedia, however, the viewer can create their own paths, starting at one place and ending at a different place each time.

The message, therefore, becomes customized to a certain degree.

personalization of mass-market information

Multimedia is not print. Designers cannot merely translate a piece written for print media to multimedia and expect it to function as well. Multimedia has many additional constraints like screen real estate, typography resolution and emitted light versus reflective.

Different ideas need to emerge to take full advantage of the **Sound-motion work needs to be** benefits of multimedia. Expectations need to change **designed from the ground up** to exploit the non-linear paths of multimedia's **read-browse-access** future. To do so, designer's must understand how information is delivered in digital environments.

Multimedia is a more fluid environment than print. In addition to having access from section to section (**leaps**) there are hypertext links that allow viewers to access related information in layers (**links**) This method of access, of being able to explore various leaps and links, allows for more than just interactivity— it creates editable environments.

With smart agents, this **customization** will advance to another level. Smart agents will access multimedia environments and pull out information that the viewer pre-specifies based on reading habits, interests and needs. Other non-specified information will remain accessible but backgrounded.

The result is the **personalization of mass-market information**, which of course has its pluses and minuses. On the one hand, viewers will be able to filter out the noise (advertisements, yellow journalism, direct-market crap) but on the other, that same viewer can isolate themselves with only information that they agree with, ignoring other's viewpoints, input or even criticism. At stake could be the democratic process— but, that may be a digression of sorts.

Given that, it is up to the designer to provide the tools to navigate and the content to explore in multimedia— the viewer takes it from there.

But the design of the interface becomes especially important, given all this **navigability, customization, & filtering of information.**

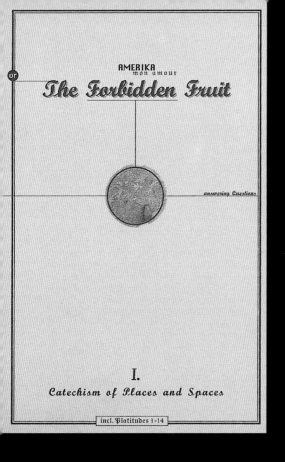

AMERIKA
mon amour

The Forbidden Fruit

or

answering Questions

I.
Catechism of Places and Spaces

incl. Platitudes 1-14

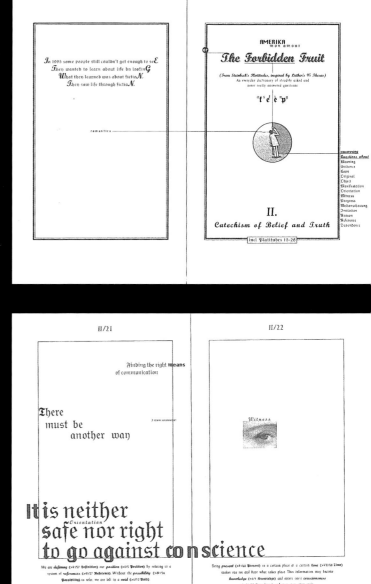

In 1995 some people still couldn't get enough to seE
Then wanted to learn about life bn lootinG
What they learned was about fictioN
Then saw life through fictioN.

romantics

AMERIKA
mon amour

The Forbidden Fruit

(from Steinbeck's Platitudes, inspired by Luther's 95 Theses)
An everyday dictionary of steadily asked and
never really answered questions

"t⁵ é è ⁸p⁸"

answering
Questions about
Meaning
Evidence
Icon
Original
Object
Manifestation
Orientation
Witness
Progress
Weltanschauung
Imitation
Reason
Reference
Dependence

II.
Catechism of Belief and Truth

incl. Platitudes 15-28

II/21

Finding the right means
of communication

There
must be
another way

It is neither
Orientation
safe nor right
to go against conscience

We are *defining* (>I/52 Definition) our *position* (>I/5 Position) by relating to a
system of *references* (>I/27 Reference). Without the possibility (>IV/14
Possibility) to refer, we are left in a *void* (>I/72 Void)

II/22

Witness

Being *present* (>X/68 Present) in a certain place at a certain *time* (>VII/58 Time)
makes one see and hear what takes place. This information may become
knowledge (>I/5 Knowledge) and enters one's consciousness
(>VI/77 Conscience) and may even alter one's
position (>I/5 Position)

III/35

Ein Zeichen sind wir, deutungslos
A sign we are, without meaning
Schmerzlos sind wir und haben fast
without pain we are and have nearly lost
Die Sprache in der Fremde verloren
our language in foreign lands

Nature

What is unnatural to a *being* (>VII/89 Being) which is able to reinvent its nature?
The artificial becomes our second nature which *distances* (>II/44 Distance)
us from our nature as a sign of human *progress*
(>II/21 Progress)

III/36

Confusion

I
Can't
Believe
It
Not
Another
Sex

Being perplexed by the signs of our *reality* (>VI/73 Reality) is no *reason* (>II/26
Reason) to become worried, since it won't take too long until we either
understand (>VI/77 Understanding) their *messages*
(>I/4 Message), or accept them as new
values (>I/58 Value)

Amerika Mon Amour or the Forbidden Fruit

Cover and spreads from a thesis project
Carolyn Steinbeck

WRITER/DESIGNER
PRINCIPAL TYPEFACES   Wittenberg, Fraktur, Script Bold, Chicago

Cranbrook Academy of Art
USA, 1995

The thesis, subtitled "An everyday dictionary of steadily asked and never really answered questions", takes the form of seven self-published booklets – "chatechisms" of places and spaces, of belief and truth, of experiences, of driving forces, of women and men, of influences and of conclusions. The booklets frame 95 cross-referenced platitudes – one per page – inspired by the 95 theses arguing against the sale of indulgences nailed to the church door in sixteenth-century Wittenberg by Martin Luther.

*t kt·le

where density and legibility are
purely dictated by how long
your finger is on the key

: a fusion of

contact

'its sensorial, sensual
value for us

what we currently create
is language that only
exists in a non-
digital space, visible only
on the simulated world of
the screen

monitor

*jean baudrillard

*try and touch
what you see*

Taktile

Wall panels for a typeface project

WRITER/DESIGNER / Ben Tibbs
PROGRAMMING ASSISTANCE / Tony Side
PRINCIPAL TYPEFACES / Taktile, Helvetica

Royal College of Art
Great Britain, 1995

neutral carrier

sterilizer

literacy will become learning to type on a keyboard

Digital technology and the keyboard have had a profound effect on the physical nature of writing. The emotional directness of mark-making on a surface has been reduced to the uniform pressing of a key. Taktile is an attempt to restore the physicality of writing by combining the tangible and the digital: the longer your finger rests on a key, the more impact it will make on the character's density and legibility.

Irony
Mediate

Broadsheets from "Lexicon" project
DESIGNER | Weston Bingham
PRINCIPAL TYPEFACES | Caecilia, VAG Rounded, Rotis Sans, State, Dr No

California Institute of the Arts
U.S.A, 1994

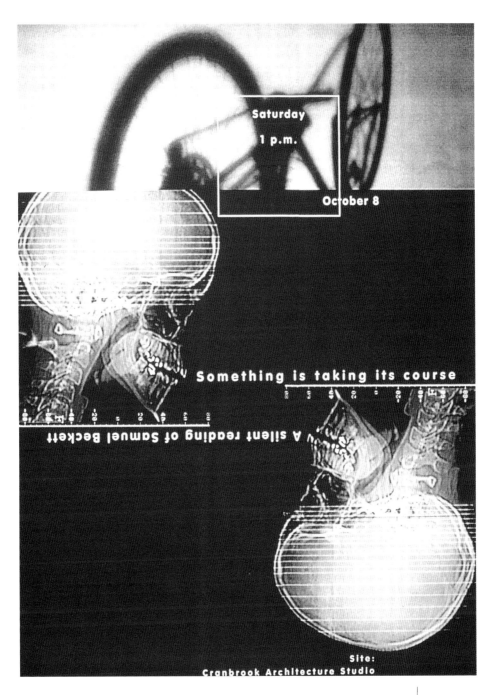

Beckett #1

Poster for a performance based
on Samuel Beckett's *Endgame*
Jeremy Francis Mende, Jeff Talbot
VAG Rounded
Jeff Talbot

DESIGNERS
PRINCIPAL TYPEFACE
CLIENT

Cranbrook Academy of Art
USA, 1995

Ask Yourself Why

Concert poster
DESIGNER | Michael Worthington
PRINCIPAL TYPEFACE | Letter Gothic
CLIENT | Dance School

California Institute of the Arts
USA, 1993

b+w

a season of explorations into black and white
30 June - 3 July 20.00 hrs
ICA institute of contemporary arts, the mall london sw1
box office 0171 930 3647

S U T **O** R E

HOW IS IT
how is it that WHAT WE KNOW
who we are WHO WE ARE

b+w a season of explorations into black and white
27 June - 23 July 11.00 18.00, 20.00
ICA/b.C.W opns (?)
ICA institute of contemporary arts the mall london sw1
box office 0171 930 3647

Suture

Poster project
DESIGNER / Vivienne Cherry
PHOTOGRAPHER / Annelise Howard Phillips
PRINCIPAL TYPEFACES / Custom-made for the project

Royal College of Art
Great Britain, 1995

Written in black and white

THE WORLDS OF WHITENESS AND BLACKNESS.

ROW UPON ROW OF
CALF-BOUND THOUGHT

GORMENGHAST

THE ANCIENT WORD

THE LONG SHELVES SURROUNDED THEM, TIER UPON TIER, CIRCUMSCRIBING THEIR WORLD
WITH A WALL OF OTHER WORLDS IMPRISONNED YET BREATHING AMONG THE NETWORK OF A
MILLION COMMAS, SEMI-COLONS, FULL STOPS, HYPHENS, AND EVERY OTHER SORT OF
PRINTED SYMBOL

SAVING SEPULCHRAVE AND TITUS WHOSE WORLDS ARE STILL
LIMITED TO THE WORLDS OF WHITENESS AND BLACKNESS

MERVYNE PEAKE

THE LONG SHELVES SURROUNDED THEM, TIER UPON TIER, CIRCUMSCRIBING THEIR
WORLD WITH A WALL OF OTHER WORLDS IMPRISONNED YET BREATHING AMONG THE
NETWORK OF A MILLION COMMAS, SEMI-COLONS, FULL STOPS, HYPHENS, AND EVERY
OTHER SORT OF PRINTED SYMBOL

IT WAS DECREED IN THE OLD TOMES
AND WAS LAW

Titus Groan

Poster project
DESIGNER / Vivienne Cherry
PRINCIPAL TYPEFACES / Custom-made for the project

Royal College of Art
Great Britain, 1995

, one needs to have

"...a smudge that will not go away."

Gérard de Nerval

open:microphone

such as the eye or the ear.

Monday
April 12
3:30

during coffe house

poetry prose performance

of nerve,

Open Microphone: A Smudge

Poster announcing an open reading on campus
DESIGNER   Brian Schorn
TYPEFACES   Trade Gothic, Snell Roundhand
CLIENT   Open Microphone Series

Open Microphone: Resonances

Poster announcing an open reading on campus
DESIGNER Brian Schorn
PRINCIPAL TYPEFACES Courier, Weiss
CLIENT Open Microphone Series

Cranbrook Academy of Art
USA, 1993

Open Microphone: Gates of Hell

Poster announcing an open reading on campus
DESIGNER Brian Schorn
PRINCIPAL TYPEFACES Cochin, Ocraelliot Black, Century Schoolbook
CLIENT Open Microphone Series

Cranbrook Academy of Art
USA, 1993

The Miles Modern Poetry Series
at the Department of English,
Wayne State University
presents
a

READiNG

by

postmo

dernis

t No

vel

is

t

kAthy Acker

Wednesday
FebruAry 2
1994

8
PM

46 Lower DeRoy
5203 Cass Ave.
(behind the Prentis Bldg. across from the Detroit Public Library)

design: Brian Schorn

FREE ADMiSSiON

Kathy Acker: Postmodern Novelist

Poster announcing a reading
DESIGNER / Brian Schorn
PRINCIPAL TYPEFACE / Serifa

Trust (105 Minutes)

Film poster
DESIGNER Brian Schorn
PRINCIPAL TYPEFACES Charlemagne, Avenir
CLIENT Sunday Night Film Series

Faculty Show

Poster
DESIGNER Michael Worthington
PRINCIPAL TYPEFACES Wood Type, Dead History, Compacta

California Institute of the Arts
USA, 1995

70s Party

Poster
DESIGNER Michael Worthington
PRINCIPAL TYPEFACES Fellaparts, Wedgie
CLIENT Student Council

California Institute of the Arts
USA, 1994

AT CALIFORNIA INSTITUTE OF THE ARTS

WE'RE **PROUD to PRESENT**

for the perusal of their Esteemed Patrons

{THE ALMOST CERTAINLY SOON TO BE FAMOUS}

PATTY DANCE

FEATURING FOUR STUPENDOUSLY MAGNIFICENT MELODIOUS CHOREOGRAPHED DANCES

MAIN GALLERY

ADMI$$ION
ABSOLUTELY
POSITIVELY
100%
FREE

IT'S A BFA THESIS SHOW! WOW

AMUSEMENT ENOUGH FOR ALL!

DON'T GO HOME! "QUARTET"

THURSDAY & FRIDAY & SATURDAY

APRIL 6th 7th 8th

8 PM

CHOREOGRAPHED BY
PATRICK LEWIS BRADBURY

NEW HOURS OF PLEASURE NEW MAD CAP FROLICS NEW STRANGE MUSIC NEW FREE SPLENDORS NEW THINGS FROM EVERYWHERE NEW BEDAZZLING COSTUMES

IT'S PATRICK, THE INCREDIBLE PIERCED BOY FROM TATUM

PRODUCED BY MEGAN GRAHAM

NEW LOFTY DANCERS NEW MID— AIR FEATS NEW GRAND CREATIONS NEW JOYS FOR ALL NEW LEAPS OF WONDER NEW THRILLS A'PLENTY NEW SENSATIONAL MOVES
NEW EXOTIC ANIMALS AND NEW FREE FOOD

RECEPTION AFTER SATURDAY'S SHOW
FOOD & DRINK & MUCH, MUCH MORE
DON'T MISS THIS SHOW! YOU'LL REGRET IT!

Patty Dance

Dance Poster
DESIGNER   Deborah Littlejohn
PRINCIPAL TYPEFACES   Matrix, Hubba Bubba, Suburban, Koo Koo

California Institute of the Arts
USA, 1995

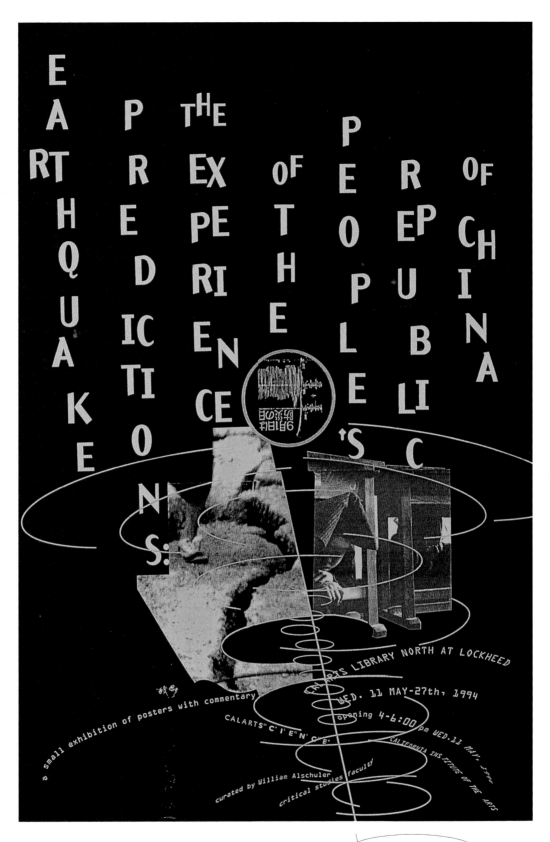

Earthquake Predictions

Exhibition poster
DESIGNER Deborah Littlejohn
PRINCIPAL TYPEFACES Barry Sans, OCRA
CLIENT Critical Studies Department

California Institute of the Arts
USA, 1994

Mike Kelley

Poster announcing a lecture
DESIGNERS Deborah Littlejohn, Shawn McKinney
PRINCIPAL TYPEFACE Arbitrary Sans
CLIENT Visiting Artist Program

California Institute of the Arts
USA, 1993

The designers scanned in many elements
and dragged them together to create a
succession of alternative designs. Believing
the poster to be finished, they pulled back
to discover that the scattered typographic
matter on the pasteboard more closely
reflected the artist's attitude than their
careful composition.

SILVERE LOTRINGER

Silvere Lotringer is a writer, critic and editor of Semiotext(e) based in New York, where he teaches at Columbia University's French Department.

"the empire of evil"

thursday march 16 6 pm LANGLEY

Silvere Lotringer

Poster announcing a le
DESIGNER Geoff McFetridge
PRINCIPAL TYPEFACES Tear, Citizen
CLIENT Visiting Artist Progra

*California Institute of the
USA, 1995*

Room 6100

contributors:

A.P.L.A.
TOM OF FINLAND (L.A.)
STUDENT AFFAIRS/
NURSE AUDREE
TOM BOGOSHIAN
MARIA'S DELI
INTERNATIONAL LIQUORS
SUNRISE DELI
GOOD VIBRATIONS
TRADER JOES
DRAKE'S
A DIFFERENT LIGHT

performers:

DANNI BABCOCK
STIFF GRIFF
JILL ST. JAQUES
SERAFINA KLARWEIN
MAHALCHICK
MANDREW
JULIANNA PARR
THE PEZ BROTHERS
MICKI PUCKERSTAR
THOR

RAFFLE
PERFORMANCES
TRASH DRAG-MART
SISSY SPACE CAFE
D.J.s
DRAG-BACKSTAGE

sissy space

AN EVENING OF DRAG CABARET

OCTOBER

8 PM

COME DRESSED

8.00

8.30

9.00

12.00

-fgay-
-fleabian-
-fbi-sexualt-
-ftranspendert-
-fstraightt-
-ftransvestitet-
-fbtightt-

OPEN BAR/TICKETS

PERFORMANCES

Sissy Space

Poster for an evening of gay cabaret
DESIGNER Michael Worthington
PRINCIPAL TYPEFACES Sissy, Killer Klown, Dominatrix,
Koo Koo Fatboy, Suburban

California Institute of the Arts
USA, 1994

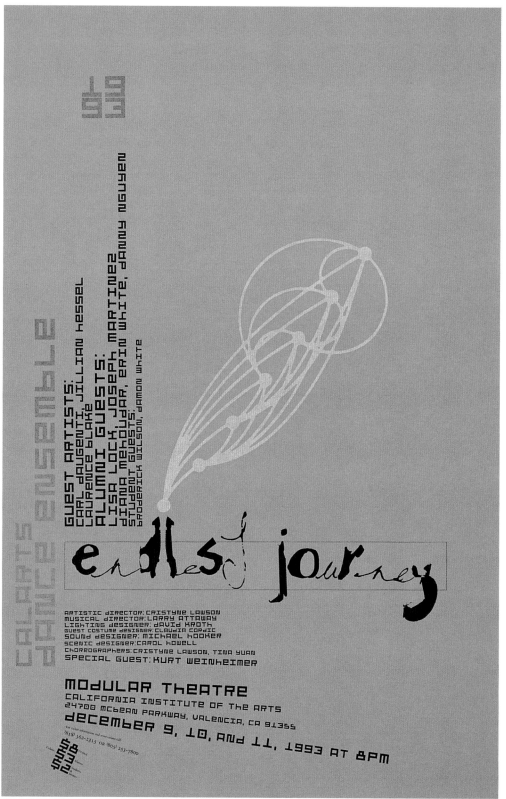

CALARTS
DANCE ENSEMBLE

1993

GUEST ARTISTS:
CARL DAUGENTI, JILLIAN KESSEL
LAURENCE BLAKE
ALUMNI GUESTS:
LISA LOCK, JOSEPH MARTINEZ
DIANA MEHOUDAR, ERIN WHITE, DANNY NGUYEN
STUDENT GUESTS:
BRODERICK WILSON, DAMON WHITE

endless journey

ARTISTIC DIRECTOR: CRISTYNE LAWSON
MUSICAL DIRECTOR: LARRY ATTAWAY
LIGHTING DESIGNER: DAVID KROTH
GUEST COSTUME DESIGNER: CLAUDIA CORDIC
SOUND DESIGNER: MICHAEL HOOKER
SCENIC DESIGNER: CAROL HOWELL
CHOREOGRAPHERS: CRISTYNE LAWSON, TINA YUAN
SPECIAL GUEST: KURT WEINHEIMER

MODULAR THEATRE
CALIFORNIA INSTITUTE OF THE ARTS
24700 MCBEAN PARKWAY, VALENCIA, CA 91355
DECEMBER 9, 10, AND 11, 1993 AT 8PM

For ticket information and reservations call
(818) 362-2315 OR (805) 253-7800

The structure of the design is
related to the general nature
of dance and to the specific
choreography of *Endless Journey*
(further referenced by the diagram
of infinity) in which dancers flowed
in and out of a trench in the stage.
The Gridlock type designed by Austin
Putman masses together to form the
"audience" for the more animated Eugenius
"dancers" designed by Worthington himself.

Endless Journey

Dance poster
DESIGNER Michael Worthington
PRINCIPAL TYPEFACES Gridlock, Eugenius
CLIENT Dance School

California Institute of the Arts
USA, 1993

214

Melding: Humanachine

Poster project on the theme of cyberspace
Margo Johnson
Hybrid digital typefaces

DESIGNER
PRINCIPAL TYPEFACES

California Institute of the Arts
USA, 1993

8/8
TYPE IS MEANT TO BE READ. There can be no deviation from that one elemental truth. the client asks little more from advertising than to have it sell the product. You can incorporate all the mood in the world throw in a dash of personality to lend it zest and stir it with an abstract idea. but, if the product doesn't sell, your brain child will fail as flat as a chef's first cake. Readability of the sales message, then, must be our first consideration

14/14
TYPE IS MEANT TO BE READ. There can be no deviation from that one elemental truth. the client asks little more from advertising than to have it sell the product. You can incorporate all the mood in the world throw in a dash of

30/30
TYPE IS MEANT TO BE READ. There can be no deviation from that one elemental truth

48/48
TYPE IS MEANT TO BE READ. There Ca n Be No Deviation From that One Ele

Type Is Meant To Be Read There Can Be No Deviation From That One Elemental Truth.

50 POINT

CHARACTERS IN COMPLETE FONT

a b c d e f g h i j k l m n o p q r s t
u v w x y z A B C D E F G H I J K
L M N O P Q R S T U V W X Y Z
`1234567890-=[]\'.,/~!@#$%^
&*()_+{}|:"<>?¡'™£¢§¶•ªº—"'
"…æ÷'⁄°··fifl†°·,—±˝"ˇÚÆ˜¿

Type is meant to be read. There can be no deviation from that one elemental truth
1 2 3 4 5 6 7 8 9 10 11 12 13 14 15 16 17 18 19 20 21 22 23 24 25 26 27 28

8/8
TYPE IS MEANT TO BE READ. There can be no deviation from that one elemental truth.

14/14
TYPE IS MEANT TO BE READ. There can be no deviation from that one elemental truth. the client asks little more from advertising than to have it sell the product. You can incorporate all the mood in the world throw in a dash of

30/30
TYPE IS MEANT TO BE READ. There can be no deviation from that one elemental truth

48/48
TYPE IS MEANT TO BE READ. There Ca n Be No Deviation From that One Ele

Type Is Meant To Be Read. There Can Be No Deviation From That One Elemental Truth.

50 POINT

CHARACTERS IN COMPLETE FONT

a b c d e f g h i j k l m n o p q r s t
u v w x y z A B C D E F G H I J K
L M N O P Q R S T U V W X Y Z
1234567890-=[]\'.,/~!@#$%^
&*()_+{}|:"<>?¡'™£§¶•ªº—"'
"…æ÷'⁄°··fifl†°·,—±˝"ˇÚÆ˜¿

Type is meant to be read. There can be no deviation from that one elemental truth
1 2 3 4 5 6 7 8 9 10 11 12 13 14 15 16 17 18 19 20 21 22 23 24 25 26 27 28

8/8
TYPE IS MEANT TO BE READ. There can be no deviation from that one elemental truth. the client asks little more from advertising than to have it sell the product. You can incorporate all the mood in the world throw in a dash of personality to lend it zest and stir it with an abstract idea. but, if the product doesn't sell, your brain child will fail as flat as a chef's first cake. Readability of the sales message, then, must be our first consideration.

14/14
TYPE IS MEANT TO BE READ. There can be no deviation from that one elemental truth. the client asks little more from advertising than to have it sell the product. You can incorporate all the mood in the world throw in a dash of

30/30
TYPE IS MEANT TO BE READ. There can be no deviation from that one elemental truth

48/48
TYPE IS MEANT TO BE READ. There Ca n Be No Deviation From that One Ele

Type Is Meant To Be Read. There Can Be No Deviation From That One Elemental Truth.

50 POINT

CHARACTERS IN COMPLETE FONT

a b c d e f g h i j k l m n o p q r s t
u v w x y z A B C D E F G H I J K
L M N O P Q R S T U V W X Y Z
`1234567890-=[]\'.,/~!@#$%^
&*()_+{}|:"<>?¡'™£¢§¶•ªº—"'
"…æ÷'⁄°··fifl†°·,—±˝"ˇÚÆ˜¿

Type is meant to be read. There can be no deviation from that one elemental truth.
1 2 3 4 5 6 7 8 9 10 11 12 13 14 15 16 17 18 19 20 21 22 23 24 25 26 27 28

Hybrid Digital Typefaces

Cover and pages from a thesis project book
DESIGNER | Margo Johnson
PRINCIPAL TYPEFACES | Hybrid digital typefaces

California Institute of the Arts
USA, 1993

Fransan

8/8

14/14

30/30

48/48

50 POINT

CHARACTERS IN COMPLETE FONT

1 2 3 4 5 6 7 8 9 10 11 12 13 14 15 16 17 18 19 20 21 22 23 24 25 26 27 28

By applying a numerical matrix to three existing typefaces – Cooper Black, Franklin Gothic, Kuenstler Script – Johnson discovered she could produce random and unexpected letterforms. Three series of 20 new fonts were generated, each named and ordered according to the matrix. A traditional type specimen book, with an introduction and diagrams, showcases the 60 hybrid typefaces and gives the project an air of technological parody.

Michael Worthington's thesis, included on California Institute of the Arts' 25th Anniversary CD-ROM, explores the possibilities for type in the interactive medium and asks why it is so often neglected in design for the screen. Mostly typographic in content, the piece offers a fluid illustration of its own arguments that takes the viewer on a sound-and-motion journey into typography's near future.

"**BOOKS** and

interactive

Digital Luddites

fear the book
will be replaced by the
'**push button**

literacy of givens"

Just as radio didn't
kill books, and TV
didn't kill radio,
different means of
communication will
exist alongside
each other.

Race, gender and other physical
attributes are irrelevent on the
net, the interface becomes the
only-face and also the only-body.

where information is
accepted rather than
challenged.

Contrary to this is the fact that perhaps
users on the internet are due to
readier to enter into dialogue "techno
anonymity."
'**push button** and debate,

literacy of givens"

Hypertype

Screen-based thesis project
WRITER/DESIGNER Michael Worthington

California Institute of the Arts
USA, 1995

Andy Altmann *23, 24, 25, 28, 29, 40, 102, 104, 105*
Born in 1962, Andy Altmann graduated with a BA from St. Martin's School of Art, London in 1985 and received an MA from the Royal College of Art in 1987. He formed Why Not Associates with David Ellis and Howard Greenhalgh immediately after college. The company has worked with a variety of clients from both the private and public sectors, including Next Directory, the Royal Mail, Hull City Council and the Royal Academy.

Caryn Aono *176*
Born in Chicago in 1959, Caryn Aono took a Bachelor of Science in graphic design from Illinois State University in 1981. She received an MFA in graphic design from Cranbrook Academy of Art in 1985. Since 1988, she has been art director of California Institute of the Arts' Public Affairs Office and she is also on the faculty of the graphic design programme. Her work has been included in the American Center for Design's 100 Show.

Chris Ashworth *64, 65, 76, 77, 138, 139*
Born in Leeds in 1969, Chris Ashworth studied for an HND in graphic design at York College of Arts and Technology, graduating in 1990. In the same year, he set up Orange, which concentrated on youth-related projects. In 1995, he joined Neil Fletcher and Amanda Sissons to form the design team Substance. Clients include MTV and Ray Gun Publishing.

Phil Baines *134, 135*
Born in Kendal, Westmorland in 1958, Phil Baines graduated with a BA from St Martin's School of Art, London in 1985 and an MA from the Royal College of Art in 1987. In 1990, he took up a residency at the Crafts Council and, since 1991, he has taught graphic design at Central Saint Martins. His letterpress typography has appeared in several exhibitions, including "British Design: New Traditions" at the Boymans van Beuningen Museum, Rotterdam in 1989.

Jonathan Barnbrook *72, 73, 74, 75, 78, 94, 95*
Born in 1966, Jonathan Barnbrook graduated with a BA from Central Saint Martins College of Art & Design, London in 1988 and an MA from the Royal College of Art in 1990. After art school he began working in London as a freelance. He directs typography and live-action commercials through Tony Kaye Films. His typefaces Mason and Exocet are released by Emigre Fonts. In 1996, he launched his own type foundry, Virus.

Richard Bates *84*
With partner Allen Hori, Richard Bates is co-principal of the design group Bates Hori. His work has been exhibited internationally in the 1990 touring exhibition "Cranbrook Design: The New Discourse" and at the Design Museum, London and the GGG Gallery, Tokyo. He has received recognition in the *I.D. Annual Design Review* and the American Center for Design's 100 Show.

Weston Bingham *200*
Born in 1968, Weston Bingham completed a BFA at the Pratt Institute in Brooklyn. After professional experience with Chermayeff & Geismar in New York, he began graduate studies at California Institute of the Arts.

Andrew Blauvelt *150, 151*
Born in 1964, Andrew Blauvelt received a BFA from Herron School of Art and an MFA from Cranbrook Academy of Art. He teaches at North Carolina State University and in 1995 occupied the interim chair of graphic design at Cranbrook. As a designer, he works for cultural and educational clients. In 1990, his work was exhibited in the touring exhibition "Cranbrook Design: the New Discourse" and he has received recognition in the *I.D. Annual Design Review*. He edited the *Visible Language* series "New Perspectives: Critical Histories of Graphic Design" and writes for *Emigre* and *Eye*.

Frédéric Bortolotti *120, 121*
Born in 1965, Frédéric Bortolotti studied at the Ecole Nationale des Arts Appliques and the Ecole Nationale des Beaux-Art in Paris. With his design studio vertmiroir, he has worked on projects for the Centre Pompidou, the Institut du Monde Arabe and has created corporate identities for private clients including Cofinoga. Bortolotti is founder of the Bulldozer project and publishes his own work under the name The Red Dozer.

Anne Burdick *109, 112, 113, 151*
Born in 1962, Anne Burdick graduated with an MFA from California Institute of the Arts. From 1995-96, she was assistant professor of graphic design at North Carolina State University. As well as teaching and maintaining her own practice, she has written widely about design. In 1995, she guest edited and produced *Emigre* nos. 35 and 36, "Mouthpiece: Clamor over Writing and Design".

Raul Cabra *80*
Born in Bogota, Columbia in 1964, Raul Cabra attended the School of Architecture in Caracas, Venezuela. He went on to study graphic design at California College of Arts and Crafts in San Francisco, graduating with a BFA in 1988. Cabra has worked as a senior designer at Tenazas Design in San Francisco on corporate and non-profit communication projects. In 1992, he became co-principal, with Martin Venezky, of the design group Diseño. In 1995, his work was included in the American Center for Design's 100 Show.

David Carson *12, 52, 53, 54, 55, 56, 57, 137*
Born in Corpus Christi, Texas, David Carson began his career as an art director/designer at *Transworld Skateboarding* magazine in 1983. He was art director of *Beach Culture* magazine from 1989-91 and art director of *Raygun* from 1992-95. He now divides his time between studios in New York and California. He has worked on commercials for Coca-Cola, Sega and other clients. *The End of Print: The Graphic Design of David Carson* was published in 1995. He is art director of *Speak* magazine.

Martin Carty *186, 187*
Born in 1968, Martin Carty completed a BA in graphic design at Central Saint Martins College of Art & Design, London in 1992 and an MA at the Royal College of Art in 1995. He has freelanced for Theatre de Complicite, *i-D* magazine and other clients. He is a partner with Ben Tibbs in the design team Automatic.

Vivienne Cherry *184, 185, 203*
Born in Derby in 1970, Vivienne Cherry graduated with a BA in graphic design from Brighton Polytechnic in 1992. A year later, after working as a designer at Mitchell Beazley publishers, she began an MA in graphic design at the Royal College of Art. Since 1995, she has worked as a freelance.

Scott Clum *9, 58, 59*
Born in 1964, Scott Clum studied at the Munson Williams Proctor Institute of Fine Art. He has been principal of Ride Design, based in Silverton, Oregon, since 1989. He is design director of *Bikini* magazine and, in 1991, launched his own magazine, *Blur*. His work has been recognised by the American Center for Design's 100 Show and by the Type Directors Club of New York.

Denise Gonzales Crisp *112*
Born in 1955, Denise Gonzales Crisp worked professionally for seven years before entering the graduate programme in graphic design at California Institute of the Arts. She has taught typography at Art Center College of Design and Otis College of Art and Design.

Richard Curren *20, 21*
Born in San Francisco in 1969, Richard Curren received a BFA from the University of Houston, Texas in 1993. He worked for the Houston Museum of Natural Science, designing computer-animated interactive kiosks. In 1994, he joined Jager Di Paola Kemp Design.

Zsolt Czakó *8, 142*
Born in Pécs, Hungary in 1965, Zsolt Czakó studied photography and graphic design at the Hungarian Academy of Applied Arts, Budapest from 1989-93, and undertook postgraduate studies in typography from 1993-94. In 1993, he was a co-founder of the creative workshop ART 'i csók, which undertakes projects for national and international clients. He exhibits regularly and, in 1994, was an organiser and participant in "New Typography", held in Pécs.

Michael Davies *62, 63*
Born in 1970, Michael Davies graduated from Kingston University with a BA in graphic design in 1993. Since then, he has worked at Lippa Pearce and as a designer at The Body Shop.

Barry Deck *136, 137, 144*
Born in Mount Peasant, Iowa in 1962, Barry Deck graduated with a BFA from Northern Illinois University in 1986 and an MFA from California Institute of the Arts in 1989. He has designed a number of well-known and widely distributed typefaces, including Template Gothic. He has worked for Viacom and Atlantic Records, designing for both print and screen.

Barbara De Wilde *46*
Working at Alfred A. Knopf in New York, Barbara De Wilde concentrates on the design of books and literature.

Mark Diaper *62, 63*
Born in 1967, Mark Diaper studied at Middlesex Polytechnic, graduating with a BA in graphic design. He has worked at Newell & Sorrell and Lippa Pearce for IBM, Decca, Waterstones and The Terence Higgins Trust.

Joan Dobkin *153*
After graduating with a BFA from Rhode Island School of Design and an MFA from the School of the Art Institute of Chicago, Joan Dobkin's main interest lay in painting and drawing. She later began a freelance career in design and completed an MFA at Cranbrook Academy of Art. She is assistant professor of graphic design at Ohio University and also maintains a freelance practice.

Elliott Peter Earls *60, 61, 172, 173, 174, 175*
Born in 1965, Elliott Peter Earls studied for an MFA at Cranbrook Academy of Art before gaining professional experience at De Harak and Poulin Associates and Elektra Records in New York. Through his company the Apollo Program, based in Greenwich, Connecticut, he releases typefaces and CD-ROMs. He has worked for Master Card International, Sony Records, the Voyager Company and *Plazm*.

Birgit Eggers *63*
Born in 1968, Birgit Eggers was educated at the F. H. Hamburg, graduating in 1993. Since then, she has worked as a freelance, first in London and from 1995 in Amsterdam. Her clients include the publishers Hamlyn.

David Ellis *23, 24, 25, 28, 29, 40, 102, 104, 105*
Born in 1962, David Ellis graduated with a BA from St. Martin's School of Art, London in 1985 and received an MA from the Royal College of Art in 1987. He formed Why Not Associates with Andy Altmann and Howard Greenhalgh immediately after college. The company has worked with a variety of clients from both the private and public sectors, including Next Directory, the Royal Mail, Hull City Council and the Royal Academy.

Stephen Farrell *96, 179, 180, 181*
Born in 1968, Stephen Farrell gained a Bachelor of Science degree in industrial design from Ohio State University. He is a proponent of visual/verbal integration, which he explores in contributions to the literary and arts journal *Private Arts*. He is a full-time faculty member in the graphic design/digital imaging department of Ray College of Design in Chicago. His fonts are distributed by [T-26].

Andrea Fella *176*
Born in 1969, Andrea Fella studied design and twentieth-century culture at the University of Michigan. She worked for the Los Angeles-based firm ReVerb for four years. In 1995, she became associate art director of *I.D.* magazine.

Edward Fella 15, 106, 162, 163, 164, 165
Born in Detroit, Michigan in 1938, Edward Fella practised commercial art and design for many years before entering Cranbrook Academy of Art in 1985. Since graduating with an MFA, he has worked for a number of cultural clients and currently teaches on the graphic design programme at California Institute of the Arts.

Detlef Fiedler 101, 114, 115, 116, 117
Born in 1955, Detlef Fiedler is a member of the Berlin design group Cyan. The group view themselves as avant-garde in the traditional sense. Designing books, posters and magazines, they have so far worked exclusively for clients in the cultural sector.

Neil Fletcher 64, 65, 139
Born in 1969, Neil Fletcher studied graphic design at Hook College of Art and Technology from 1987-89. In 1991, he established Pd-p, working for Sheffield University Union of Students and other clients. In 1995, he joined Chris Ashworth and Amanda Sissons to form the design team Substance. Clients include MTV and Ray Gun Publishing.

Barbara Glauber 122, 123, 160, 161
Born in Buffalo, New York in 1962, Barbara Glauber received an MFA from California Institute of the Arts. She teaches at the Cooper Union, New York and is a critic on the graphic design programme at Yale University. She has a New York-based design studio and concentrates on publication design and information graphics for educational and cultural clients. In 1993, she curated the exhibition "Lift and Separate: Graphic Design and the Quote Unquote Vernacular" at the Cooper Union.

Heike Grebin 100
Born in Rostock in 1959, Heike Grebin studied architecture at the Hochschule für Architektur und Bauwesen in Weimar and went on to work as an architect for four years. In the late 1980s, she worked as a typographer for a children's book publisher and in 1990 she joined Grappa, the Berlin design group. Grappa are committed to working on low budgets for cultural institutions and many of their clients are based in East Berlin's historic centre.

April Greiman 18, 19
Born in 1948, April Greiman graduated with a BFA from Kansas City Art Institute in 1970 and pursued graduate studies at the Design School in Basel from 1970-71. Her Los Angeles-based practice, known for its pioneering use of technology, is involved with interactive and multimedia projects, as well as graphic, motion and environmental design. A former director of the visual communications programme at California Institute of the Arts, she serves as graduate adviser for Art Center College of Design, Pasadena and is an instructor at the Southern California Institute of Architecture. A one-woman exhibition was staged at the Arc en Rêve Centre d'Architecture, Bordeaux, France in 1994 and subsequently toured.

Julian Harriman-Dickinson 86
Born in 1972, Julian Harriman-Dickinson studied graphic design, graduating with a BA. He has worked for Lowe Howard-Spink as a designer/typographer. He won a D&AD gold award while still a student.

Daniela Haufe 101, 114, 115, 116, 117
Born in 1966, Daniela Haufe is a member of the Berlin design group Cyan. The group view themselves as avant-garde in the traditional sense. Designing books, posters and magazines, they have so far worked exclusively for clients in the cultural sector.

Andrew Henderson 26, 27
Born in New York in 1967, Andrew Henderson graduated from Minneapolis College of Art and Design in 1995. He assisted Jan Jancourt on the redesign of the *Utne Reader* and is the magazine's associate art director.

Allen Hori 33, 177
With partner Richard Bates, Allen Hori is co-principal of the design group Bates Hori. His work has been exhibited internationally in the 1990 touring exhibition "Cranbrook Design: The New Discourse" and at the Design Museum, London and the GGG Gallery, Tokyo. He has received recognition in the *I.D. Annual Design Review* and the American Center for Design's 100 Show.

Karl Hyde 140, 141
Born in England in 1957, Karl Hyde graduated from art school with a BA in sculpture, installation and video. In 1980, he formed the rock group Freur with John Warwicker and Richard Smith. With Smith and Darren Emerson, he launched Underworld. He is a member of the design collective Tomato.

Jan Jancourt 26, 27, 150
Born in Minnesota in 1957, Jan Jancourt studied for a Bachelor of Science in design at Bemidji State Univerisity from 1977-81. He completed an MFA at Cranbrook Academy of Art in 1985. He was an intern at Studio Dumbar and, since 1986, has been associate professor at Minneapolis College of Art and Design, while pursuing a freelance career with projects for the Walker Art Center and other clients. His work was exhibited in "Holland in Form: Dutch Design 1945-87" at the Stedelijk Museum and in the 1990 touring exhibition, "Cranbrook Design: The New Discourse".

Damian Jaques 124, 125
Born in 1965, Damian Jaques completed a BA in fine art at Portsmouth Polytechnic in 1988, and an MA in print-making at Wimbledon School of Art in 1991.

Alicia Johnson 53
Born in 1960, Alicia Johnson studied at Hutchins School, a liberal arts programme at the UC Sonoma. She is president and co-director of Johnson & Wolverton, based in Portland, Oregon. The company's clients include Amnesty International, The Democratic National Committee, the AVIA Group International and Ray Gun Publishing.

Andrew Johnson 89, 103
Born in Essex in 1968, Andrew Johnson was educated at Brighton Polytechnic, graduating with a BA in 1990, and at the Royal College of Art, graduating with an MA in 1992. As a freelance, his clients have included the Institute of Contemporary Arts, the London Ecology Centre and RTZ Corporation. He has collaborated with Nick Oates on theatre publicity material. In 1995, he became art director of *Blueprint* magazine.

Margo Johnson 108, 188, 215, 216, 217
Born in Toledo, Ohio in 1964, Margo Johnson followed a BFA from the University of Michigan with an MFA at California Institute of the Arts. Since graduating in 1993, she has worked in Los Angeles in a variety of media for clients in the music industry and television. She teaches design and typography at Otis College of Art and Design. Her *Hybrid Digital Typefaces* project was included in the American Center for Design's 100 Show.

Jason Kedgley 49
Born in 1969, Jason Kedgley gained a BA in graphic design from the London College of Printing and an MA from Central Saint Martins College of Art & Design. He is a member of the design collective Tomato.

Jeffery Keedy 108, 122, 183, 188, 189
Born in Battle Creek, Michigan in 1957, Jeffery Keedy gained a BFA in graphic design and photography at Western Michigan University in 1981. After a period of professional experience in Boston and Honolulu, he studied for an MFA at Cranbrook Academy of Art, graduating in 1985. He moved to Los Angeles to teach at California Institute of the Arts and was director of its graphic design programme from 1991-95. A polemical post-modernist in his writings, he is a regular contributor to design publications such as *Emigre* and *Eye*. In 1991, his typeface Keedy Sans was released by Emigre Fonts. In 1996, he launched a number of new faces through his type foundry, Cipher.

Chip Kidd 47
Born in 1964, Chip Kidd was educated at Pennsylvania State University, graduating with a BA in graphic design in 1986. Since then, he has worked as a book jacket designer at Alfred A. Knopf in New York. His designs have been included in the American Center for Design's 100 Show for five years running. In addition to coverage in the design press, his work has been featured in *Time* magazine and *The New York Times*.

Somi Kim 66, 67, 156, 157, 160, 161, 176
Born in 1962, Somi Kim gained a BA from Harvard University in 1984 and an MFA from California Institute of the Arts in 1989. In 1990, she was a founding partner of ReVerb, a Los Angeles-based design firm whose clients range from grass-roots community centres to corporations, museums and foundations. She is a graduate adviser for Art Center College of Design, Pasadena and a visiting lecturer at Cranbrook Academy of Art and other schools.

Doug Kisor 154, 155
Born in Mason, Michigan in 1949, Doug Kisor has been working in design education since he completed an MFA in graphic design at Michigan University in 1984. He is director of the graphic design studies programme at Eastern Michigan University. His work has been included in the *AIGA Annual* and the American Center for Design's 100 Show. He is working with the Graphic Design Education Association to develop international exchange programmes and has co-developed the Rotterdam-based de Program, which hosts a group of international participants, who work with leading practitioners, theorists and educators.

Jacques Koeweiden 128, 129
Born in 1957, Jacques Koeweiden studied at the Royal Academy of Art and Design in Den Bosch from 1978-83. In 1985, he became art director of *Vinyl* magazine and in 1986 he formed Koeweiden Postma with Paul Postma. The company works for international corporate and cultural clients, including Chiat/Day, Glaxo, the Hogeschule of Amsterdam, the Royal Dutch PTT, UNICEF and Nike. They received a gold award in the 1993 Typography International Awards and were featured in the "Dutch Design" exhibition at the Design Museum, London in 1991.

Susan Lally 126
After completing a BFA in painting at the University of Illinois in 1983, Susan Lally went on to graduate studies in graphic design at Cranbrook Academy of Art. She has worked as a freelance designer with various design groups in Chicago and designs for a variety of media with Zun Design. Her work was included in the 1990 touring exhibition "Cranbrook Design: the New Discourse" and she has received recognition in the American Center for Design's 100 Show and *How* magazine's *International Annual of Design*.

Susan LaPorte 92, 169
Born in 1965, Susan LaPorte received a BFA from the University of Illinois, Chicago and an MFA from California Institute of the Arts. In the early 1990s, she worked as an intern at CalArts and the Walker Art Center. Since 1993, she has been assistant professor of graphic design at Eastern Michigan University. Her typefaces were used in the first five issues of *Raygun* and have also appeared in *Emigre*. She was included in the American Center for Design's 100 Show in 1993 and 1995.

George LaRou 123, 169, 170, 171
Born in Maine, George LaRou received an MFA from California Institute of the Arts in 1990. He taught for four years at Eastern Michigan University and is an associate professor at Maine College of Art. His work has been featured in the American Center for Design's 100 Show in 1994 and 1995, and in the exhibition "Lift and Separate" at the Cooper Union, New York in 1993.

Dominic Lippa *62*

Born in 1962, Dominic Lippa studied graphic design at London College of Printing from 1981-84. He worked at Smith & Milton, Michael Thierens and Newell & Sorrell, before setting up Lippa Pearce Design with Harry Pearce and Giles Calver in 1990. He was art director of *Baseline* for five years. Clients include the Royal Mail, Boots the Chemist and Waitrose. He is on the executive committee of London's Typographic Circle and has judged the RSA Student Awards for three years.

Deborah Littlejohn *209, 210, 211*

Born in Raleigh, North Carolina in 1966, Deborah Littlejohn graduated with a BFA in design from Western Carolina University in 1992. She completed an MFA at California Institute of the Arts in 1994. She has worked for ReVerb in Los Angeles and led an Internet workshop at CalArts. She is a designer in the Walker Art Center's design department.

Whitney Lowe *66, 67, 156, 157, 176*

Born in 1958, Whitney Lowe was educated at California Polytechnic State University and Art Center College of Design, Pasadena, graduating in 1982. He worked for Knoll International and Anthon Beeke's studio in Amsterdam before, in 1990, becoming a founding partner of ReVerb, a Los Angeles-based design firm whose clients range from grass-roots community centres to corporations, museums and foundations.

Kevin Lyons *212*

Born in 1969, Kevin Lyons graduated from Rhode Island School of Design with a BFA in film in 1988. He recently completed an MFA at California Institute of the Arts.

Seònaid MacKay *184, 185*

Born in 1970, Seònaid MacKay studied graphic design at Glasgow School of Art, graduating with a BA in 1993, and at the Royal College of Art, graduating with an MA in 1995. She is a designer/film-maker and has exhibited at the Edinburgh Film Festival and Cherbourgh Film Festival. She works for Simple Productions, a graphic and moving-image production company.

P. Scott Makela *30, 31, 32, 78, 79, 97, 145*

Born in St. Paul, Minnesota in 1960, P. Scott Makela took a degree in political science before completing a BFA in visual communication at Minneapolis College of Art and Design in 1984. From 1989-91, he studied for an MFA in graphic design at Cranbrook Academy of Art. His first business venture was Makela + Knickelbine Design in Los Angeles. Words and Pictures for Business and Culture, his current venture, is a "multi-aspect" company dealing with advanced design technologies. Clients include Warner Brothers Records, Nike and PBS. He worked as a consultant on the 1990 touring exhibition "Cranbrook Design: The New Discourse". In 1996, he was appointed joint chair (with Laurie Haycock Makela) of the graphic design programme at Cranbrook Academy of Art.

Geoff McFetridge *7, 212*

Born in 1971, Geoff McFetridge worked as a freelance designer for snowboard and skateboard companies between studies at Alberta College of Art in Calgary, Canada and California Institute of the Arts. He completed his MFA in 1995.

Shawn McKinney *189, 211*

Born in 1960, Shawn McKinney majored in liberal arts/English at Tulane University, graduating with a BA in 1982. He started at the Texan design firm of Fuller, Dyal and Stamper as a copywriter, leaving four years later as a senior level graphic designer. He completed an MFA in graphic design at California Institute of the Arts in 1992. In 1995, he became a lecturer in computer graphic design at Wanganui Regional Community Polytechnic in New Zealand.

Jeremy Francis Mende *192, 193, 201*

After gaining a first degree in psychology at UCLA in 1991, Jeremy Francis Mende worked as an art director on various magazines. In 1995, he completed an MFA in graphic design at Cranbrook Academy of Art. He was an intern at Studio Dumbar in 1994.

Rebeca Méndez *152, 158, 159*

Born in 1962, Rebeca Méndez graduated from Art Center College of Design, Pasadena in 1984. She worked for several design firms in Los Angeles before rejoining the college as its designer in 1989. She is now its design director, a post that involves both teaching and practice. She was awarded designer of the year in both 1991 and 1992 by The Council for the Advancement and Support of Education and her work has appeared in the American Center for Design's 100 Show and the *I.D.'s Annual Design Review*. Her designs are included in the permanent collections of the Library of Congress, the Cooper-Hewitt, National Design Museum and the Getty Center.

Jennifer Moody *98*

Born in 1965, Jennifer Moody graduated from Western Michigan University with a BFA and went on to complete an MFA at California Institute of the Arts in 1993. She worked in Chicago as a designer at Cagney & McDowell and ABC-TV. In 1993, she took a position in CalArts' Office of Public Affairs. Her work has been selected for the American Center for Design's 100 Show. She is a partner with Gail Swanlund in the Los Angeles design firm Nice.

James Moore *66, 67*

Born in 1971, James Moore graduated from California Institute of the Arts with a BFA in 1993. He works as a designer at the Los Angeles-based design firm ReVerb.

Patrick Morrissey *24, 25, 28, 29, 104, 105*

Born in 1972, Patrick Morrissey studied graphic design at the London College of Printing, graduating with a BA in 1994. He freelances for Why Not Associates in London.

Roelof Mulder *132, 133*

After studying fine art at the Arnhem Institute for the Arts, Roelof Mulder founded a gallery, released an artist's book, *Speed is what we need*, and exhibited paintings and sculptures internationally. He became involved in interior and fashion design in the early 1990s and began to work full time as a graphic designer in 1992. His clients include the Dutch Red Cross and the Stedelijk Museum, Amsterdam. He won the Rotterdam Design Prize in 1993. Since 1994, he has taught graphic design at the Arnhem Institute and, in 1995, he became an editor and designer of the Dutch architectural quarterly *Forum*.

Robert Nakata *10, 41, 42, 43, 44, 45*

Born in Toronto in 1960, Robert Nakata attended the Ontario College of Art from 1979-83. After working as a designer in Canada for two years, he completed an MFA at Cranbrook Academy of Art in 1985. He has worked for design firms in the United States and the Netherlands, including McCoy & McCoy in Michigan and Studio Dumbar in the Hague. He is now with Wieden & Kennedy in Amsterdam. His work was included in the 1990 touring show "Cranbrook Design: The New Discourse" and more recently in "Displaced Voices", a two-person show with Allen Hori at DDD Gallery, Osaka, Japan.

Lisa Nugent *66, 67, 143, 156, 157*

Born in 1955, Lisa Nugent was educated at California State University, Long Beach and California Institute of the Arts, graduating with an MFA in 1988. In 1990, she was a founding partner of ReVerb, a Los Angeles-based design firm whose clients range from grass-roots community centres to corporations, museums and foundations. From 1990-94, she taught experimental design and computer typography at Otis College of Art and Design. In 1993, she was a juror for the Type Directors Club of New York awards.

Nick Oates *89*

Born in 1968, Nick Oates was educated at Central Saint Martins College of Art & Design, London, graduating with a BA in 1990, and at the Royal College of Art, graduating with an MA in 1992. As a student, he was an intern at Hard Werken Design in the Netherlands. He has worked as a freelance designer in London for Diesel Jeans, Paul Smith and other clients and has collaborated with Andrew Johnson on theatre publicity material.

Susan Parr *176*

Born in 1959, Susan Parr was educated at Pacific NW College of Art and Parsons School of Design, graduating with a BFA in 1986. For four years she had her own graphic design studio. In 1990, she was a founding partner of ReVerb, a Los Angeles-based design firm whose clients range from grass-roots community centres to corporations, museums and foundations.

John Plunkett *15, 16, 34, 35, 36, 37*

After graduating with a degree in communication design from California Institute of the Arts in 1977, John Plunkett worked with Colin Forbes and Dan Friedman at Pentagram in New York. With partner Barbara Kuhr, he is responsible for the look and feel of both *Wired* magazine and *HotWired*, the first Web-based publication on the Internet. Plunkett + Kuhr's design office is based in Park City, Utah and clients include Carnegie Hall Museum and the Sundance Film Festival. In 1995, *Wired* won the National Magazine Award for design from the American Society of Magazine Editors.

Paul Postma *128, 129*

Born in 1958, Paul Postma studied at the Royal Academy of Art and Design in Den Bosch from 1979-84. He worked at Samenwerkende Ontwerpers in Amsterdam and went on to become art director of *Vinyl* magazine from 1985-86. In 1986, he formed Koeweiden Postma with Jacques Koeweiden. The company works for international corporate and cultural clients, including Chiat/Day, Glaxo, the Hogeschule of Amsterdam, the Royal Dutch PTT, UNICEF and Nike. They received a gold award in the 1993 Typography International Awards and were featured in the "Dutch Design" exhibition at the Design Museum, London in 1991.

Chris Priest *40*

Born in 1967, Chris Priest graduated from Central Saint Martins College of Art & Design, London with a BA in graphic design in 1989. He worked for Why Not Associates for several years and, in 1995, teamed up with Jo Wright to form the London-based Studio Barbara.

Pam Racs *82*

Born in 1964, Pam Racs was educated in graphic design at Art Center College of Design, Pasadena. Since 1994, she has been a designer at Johnson & Wolverton.

Paul Sahre *88, 93*

Born in 1964, Paul Sahre was educated at Kent State University, where he completed a BFA in 1987 and an MFA in 1990. From 1992-93, he worked as senior designer at Rutka Weadock, and he is now creative director of GKV Design. He maintains a freelance practice, offering his services free to the non-profit Fells Point Corner Theatre. His work was been recognised by the American Center for Design's 100 Show.

Katie Salen *118, 119*

Born in 1967, Katie Salen was educated at the University of Texas at Austin, graduating with a BFA, and at Rhode Island School of Design, graduating with an MFA in graphic design. She was assistant professor of design at the Virginia Commonwealth University and, from 1995, assistant professor in the department of art and art history at the University of Texas. She maintains a freelance practice, designing mainly for non-profit clients. Since 1993, she has been editor and designer of the design journal *Zed*. Her work has been recognised by the American Center for Design's 100 Show.

Liisa Salonen *190, 191*

An expatriate American, living in Canada, Liisa Salonen completed a Bachelor of Science in design at the University of Michigan in 1971 and undertook graduate studies at Cranbrook Academy of Art. She has worked as a designer and art director for institutional publications.

Louise Sandhaus *106, 113, 166*

After studying graphic design at California Institute of the Arts and graduating with a BFA in 1993 and an MFA in 1994, Louise Sandhaus was designer-in-residence at the Jan van Eyck Akademie, Maastricht in 1995. She has been a commercial designer since 1980, and has worked on projects with ReVerb in Los Angeles and Total Design in the Netherlands. Her work was included in the American Center for Design's 100 Show in 1995. She is designer, writer and co-publisher of the journal *Errant Bodies*.

Brian Schorn *167, 168, 182, 204, 205, 206, 207*

Born in 1961, Brian Schorn undertook two years of pre-med at Oakland University, a BFA in photography at the Center for Creative Studies, an MFA in photography at the University of Michigan, an MFA in creative writing at Brown University, and an MFA in graphic design at Cranbrook Academy of Art. While at Cranbrook, he worked as an intern for ReVerb in Los Angeles. His writing and design have been published in *Emigre* and he has been recognised by the Type Directors Club of New York.

Richard Shanks *194, 195*

After completing a bachelor's degree in graphic design and English at the University of Michigan in 1988, Richard Shanks worked in advertising. In 1990, he set up his own design practice, Visual Thinking. In 1995, he completed an MFA at California Institute of the Arts.

Laura Lacy-Sholly & James Sholly *130*

Both born in 1965, Laura Lacy-Sholly and James Sholly are partners in the design group Antenna. Clients include the Indiana Civil Liberties Union, Indianapolis Museum of Art, Stonycreek farms and Indianapolis Zoo. They were visiting artists at Cranbrook Academy of Art in 1993 and at the School of the Art Institute of Chicago in 1994. Their work was included in the American Center for the Design's 100 Show in 1992, 1993 and 1994.

Amanda Sissons *64, 65, 139*

After graduating from the London College of Printing with a BA in graphic and media design, in 1995, Amanda Sissons worked for the design group Area. In 1995, she joined Chris Ashworth and Neil Fletcher to form the design team Substance.

Carolyn Steinbeck *196, 197*

Born in 1967 in Berlin, Carolyn Steinbeck studied graphic design at Fachochschule in Darmstadt, Germany before winning a Fulbright scholarship to attend Cranbrook Academy of Art. She gained her MFA in 1995.

Shelley Stepp *189*

Born in 1950, Shelley Stepp graduated with an MFA from California Institute of the Arts in 1994. She subsequently became director of CalArts' Mac Lab for graphic design. She also works as a freelance designer for CalArts' Office of Public Affairs and other clients.

James Stoecker *188*

Born in 1963, James Stoecker completed a BFA in graphic design at Western Carolina University in 1987. He worked as an assistant art director at Whittle Communications in Tennessee for four years and, in 1993, completed an MFA at California Institute of the Arts. He works as art director at Electric Image Incorporated, Pasadena and is a part-time faculty member of the graphic design department of San Jose State University.

Gail Swanlund *108, 110*

Born in St. Paul, Minnesota in 1957, Gail Swanlund gained a BFA from the University of Minnesota in 1981. After working as a designer for several years, she completed an MFA at California Institute of the Arts in 1992. She worked for two years as a graphic designer at *Emigre* magazine and, since 1995, has taught at CalArts. She is a partner with Jennifer Moody in the Los Angeles design firm Nice.

Carlo Tartaglia *7, 22, 127*

Born in 1971, Carlo Tartaglia studied graphic design at Ravensbourne College of Design and Communication. In 1995, he completed an MA in graphic design at the Royal College of Art.

Simon Taylor *70, 71, 76, 77*

Born in 1965, Simon Taylor gained a BA in graphic design. He is a member of the design collective Tomato.

Anusch Thielbeer *99*

Born in Hamburg in 1963, Anusch Thielbeer studied industrial design at Kiel College from 1985-89. She began collaborating with the Berlin design group Grappa in 1993. Grappa are committed to working on low budgets for cultural institutions and many of their clients are based in East Berlin's historic centre.

Joseph Thomas *81, 85*

Born in Swansea, Wales in 1968, Joseph Thomas studied graphic design at Bristol Polytechnic and went on to Central Saint Martins College of Art & Design, London, graduating with an MA in 1991. He co-founded the design company Push. Clients include cultural organisations such as South West Arts and the British Film Institute.

Ben Tibbs *198, 199*

Born in 1970, Ben Tibbs studied graphic design at Glasgow School of Art, graduating with a BA in 1993, and at the Royal College of Art, graduating with an MA in 1995. In 1992, his work was including in the touring exhibition "Autogeddon" and he won the Scottish Art Director's Student Award. He has lectured in graphic design at Glasgow School of Art and Kingston University. He is a partner with Martin Carty in the design team Automatic.

Andreas Trogisch *100*

Born in Riesa in 1959, Andreas Trogisch studied exhibition design at the Fachschule für Werbung and Gestaltung from 1983-88. In 1989, he became a founder member of the design collective Grappa. The group are committed to working on low budgets for cultural institutions and many of their clients are based in East Berlin's historic centre. He has taught at the Merz-Akademie in Stuttgart and the Hdk in Berlin.

Alexei Tylevich *50, 51, 68, 69, 146, 147, 148, 149*

Born in Minsk, Belarus in 1972, Alexei Tylevich completed a BA in painting at Minsk School of Art. He went on graduate from Minneapolis College of Art and Design with a BFA in graphic design. He now lives and works in the United States. He has designed for print and screen for Sega, Airwalk Shoes and other clients. His work was selected for the American Center for Design's 100 Show in 1993.

Rick Valicenti *38, 39, 178*

Born in 1951, Rick Valicenti was educated at Bowling Green State University, graduating in with a BFA in 1973, and the University of Iowa, graduating with an MFA in photography in 1976. In 1982, he established R. Valicenti Design in Chicago and, in 1988, he set up the design group Thirst, which now operates from Barrington, Illinois. Thirstype was initiated in 1992 to release new typeface designs. He has been on the board of directors of the American Institute of Graphic Arts, chairman of the American Center for Design's 100 Show and a juror of the President's Design Awards.

Rudy VanderLans *17, 109, 110, 111*

Born in 1955, Rudy VanderLans studied graphic design at the Royal Academy of Fine Art in the Hague, graduating in 1979. After working for several years as a designer in the Netherlands, he moved to California and studied photography in the masters programme at the University of California, Berkeley. In 1984, he co-founded *Emigre*, a general arts and culture magazine. Early issues featured the digital typefaces of his partner, Zuzana Licko, and this led to the setting up of Emigre Fonts, which releases typefaces by Licko and other designers. *Emigre* itself went on to become an international forum for the new typography. Clients include Apple Computer and San Francisco's Artspace. A ten-year retrospective book, *Emigre: Graphic Design into the Digital Realm*, was published in 1994.

Martin Venezky *56, 60, 61, 80, 90*

Born in 1957, Martin Venezky attended the Hopkins Center Design Studio at Dartmouth College, New Hampshire, graduating with a BA in 1980. He worked as a designer for several years before completing an MFA at Cranbrook Academy of Art in 1993. After an internship at Studio Dumbar, he returned on graduation to work at the company. He now works in San Francisco, both independently and in partnership with Raul Cabra as Diseño. His work was included in the American Center for Design's 100 Show in 1993, 1994 and 1995.

John Warwicker *48, 76, 77, 140, 141*

Born in London in 1955, John Warwicker completed a BA in graphic design at Camberwell School of Art in 1977. In 1980, he completed an MA in visual communication at Birmingham Polytechnic, where he became involved in research into electronic interactive media. In the early 1980s, he worked with Karl Hyde and Richard Smith as a member of the rock group Freur and as a creative director at Da Gama. He became head of art and video at A&M Records and from 1987-91 he was creative director at Vivid I.D. He is a member of the design collective Tomato.

Lorraine Wild *106, 189, 176*

After studying at Yale University and Cranbrook Academy of Art, Lorraine Wild began a career as a designer of books on art, architecture and design for Rizzoli, MIT Press, the Museum of Contemporary Art in Los Angeles and other clients. She was director of the graphic design programme at California Institute of the Arts and writes about design history, theory and criticism for *Emigre*, *I.D.* and other publications. In 1990, she was a founding partner of ReVerb, a Los Angeles-based design firm whose clients range from grass-roots community centres to corporations, museums and foundations. In 1995, she left ReVerb to work as a freelance.

Cornel Windlin *11, 87, 91, 131*

Born in 1964, Cornel Windlin studied at the Schule für Gestaltung in Lucerne. He spent the late 1980s and early 1990s in London, working, among others, for Neville Brody. He now runs his own studio in Zurich. His work has been published in *Graphic Agitation* (1993) and *Wear Me* (1995).

Hal Wolverton *53, 82, 83*

Born in 1960, Hal Wolverton studied on scholarship at the University of Washington's Pratt Institute. He is president and co-director of Johnson & Wolverton, based in Portland, Oregon. The company's clients include Amnesty International, The Democratic National Committee, the AVIA Group International and Ray Gun Publishing.

Graham Wood *10, 49*

Born in Beckenham, Kent in 1965, Graham Wood completed a BA and an MA in graphic design at Central Saint Martins College of Art & Design, London. He is a member of the design collective Tomato and works in a variety of media, including print and video.

Michael Worthington *183, 202, 208, 213, 214, 218, 219*

Born in 1966, Michael Worthington graduated from Central Saint Martins College of Art & Design, London with a BA in 1991. He worked as a partner in the London-based design group Studio Dm and taught design at Central Saint Martins and Oxford Brookes University. In 1995, he completed an MFA at California Institute of the Arts. He has worked on projects for ReVerb and teaches at CalArts.